In Defense of Narcissism

The Creative Self in Search of Meaning

by Carl Goldberg, Ph.D.

Gardner Press, New York

*This book is dedicated
in memory of my father, Samuel Goldberg*

GARDNER PRESS, INC.
19 Union Square West
New York 10003

Library of Congress Cataloging in Publication Data:

Goldberg, Carl.
   In defense of narcissism.

   Bibliography: p.
   Includes index.
   1. Narcissism.   2. Self.   3. Creative ability.
4. Psychotherapy.   I. Title.
BF575.N35G64   155.2   80-15385
ISBN 0-89876-005-4

Printed in the United States of America

CONTENTS

Preface

"The correct perception of any matter and a complete misunderstanding of the matter do not wholly exclude one another."

—Franz Kafka

This is a series of essays on modern man—that which he is—with some attempt to account for how he became that way and why he has chosen, albeit, often unwittingly, to remain as he is. This is also a thesis on values and a theory of action. I endeavor in the following pages to examine the persistent search and struggle by modern man for a personal identity and a sense of meaning and purpose for his existence. In this exploration I have attempted to put foward a philosophical position that is both positive and positivistic. My position both exhorts, as well as examines on the basis of what evidence exists, what modern man may choose for himself, if he comes to terms with his human condition with courage and passion.

Each of us is called upon by the incident of our existence to answer for ourselves why we are here—why we exist. Nihilistic endeavors, even when expressed with the eloquence of a Camus (1955), fail to absolve our ontological prerequisite from our everyday experience. From moment to moment, each of us, as best we can, struggles or fails to struggle—with derivative psychological consequences—with the imperative of our existence. It is not that we are not abundantly abetted in avoiding our ontological struggle by those around us. We are continually bombarded with societal agents' notions about what our own personal purpose in existence is, should be, or must become. We are provided with easy, poultice, and saccharin answers just as we are offered difficult, if not impervious, options. It really matters not! These answers are not our own. We are required to answer the purpose of our own existence for ourselves directly and personally, that is to say, on the basis of our own experience, or we are destined to fail to know and realize ourselves, at best, to any degree to which we might hope.

I am also concerned in this volume with the interface of Self and society. In a free society the need for personal responsibility on the part of all its citizens in indispensable. Without its presence the notion of a free society remains an abstract and unrealized ideal. Of course, we are not born responsible. Nor does the process of becoming a responsible individual occur fortuitously in some persons and not in others. An enlightened attitude toward our responsibilities as social beings needs encouragement and guidance. Yet, whereas there has been considerable discussion addressed to what are desirable traits of the responsible citizen in a free society, there has been, concomitantly, appreciably far less discussion concerning the development of these attributes. To provide the ways of purposive action and enlightened philosophical perspective, which will enable the individual to become that which he seeks to be, we need more than simply explanations of why individuals choose to disregard and divest themselves of responsibility.

The task of developing personal responsibility requires exploring the meaning of Selfhood in a way rather divergent from how Self is generally discussed in the social sciences. In the essays to follow I am concerned with the creative Self, that is, a Self that is neither simply a process of mediation and reaction to historical and environmental precursors, as in the psychological view of ego, or as a collage of reflected appraisals of the person of the Self, as in the sociological view of Self. Selfhood has these aspects, of course. More importantly, however, Selfhood is an emergent and intentional endeavor. Selfhood is a personal invention, a pro-active activity in which the individual creates a world in which to exist. The world the Self interacts with has no intrinsic value or meaning, as these evaluations derive from the concert of the Self's negotiated relations with other individuals to create meaning and richness for the Self's existence. Admittedly, the notion of the creative Self has been proposed by existential and humanistic writers. Nonetheless, the specific process of developing the creative Self has been neither delineated nor carefully examined in these endeavors. As a result, the relationship of emotion, volition, intellect, action, and purpose has not been integrated into a theory of personality. In the essays to follow a theory of personality that unites the Self with its psychological functions is promulgated. This theory examines the phenomenology of the Self's awareness of possibility for purposive human action. The implications for mental health are explored within this context. A prelude to my discussion of mental health and the awareness of possibility is contained in Alan Watts's (1961) apt observation that

the normal state of consciousness in our culture is both the context and the breeding ground of mental disease. A complex of societies of vast material wealth bent on mutual destruction is anything but a condition of social health. [P. 16]

As a theory of action this volume is intended toward guiding the individual in developing an active personal and social philosophy for more fully maximizing his ability to hypothesize, test assumptions, and experiment with the conditions of his existence. This is an area of inquiry toward which Sidney Jourard (1968) has argued that the social sciences have failed to shift their attention. Jourard deplores

> how odd it seems that psychology has learned more about man at his worst than at his best.... We need psychologists with the most informed imaginations and talent for ingenious experimentation to wrestle with such questions as "What are the outer limits of human potential for transcending biological pressures, social pressures, and the impact on a person of his past conditioning? What developmental and interpersonal and situational conditions conduce to courage, creativity, transcendent behavior, love, laughter, commitments to truth, justice and virtue?" [Pp. 6–7]

Why have I written a book with the provocative title, "In Defense of Narcissism"? As the reader might surmise, I have written this volume from a struggle with my own narcissism. In abiding with the philosophical position I propose in this volume, I have written the essays to follow as much for my own edification as for that of the reader. I believe fervently what I have written, but only as tenaciously as I mistrust my own statements. A contradiction? Perhaps! But in my own interest I must question my own assumptions passionately and intellectually. Both are necessary for a meaningful commitment to my Self as a viable project of my existence. The reader should do the same for himself. What I mean is that my pen writes from a burning flame within me. I speak no objective truths, simply because I know of none. The reader who is alert to my irony must readily perceive in my describing the means for struggling for personal meaning to which I am committed that I write as authoritatively as the most zealous metaphysician and priest of other men's souls. So be it! This is my paradox and my contradiction! Like Kierkegaard, I believe that it is useless, if not impossible, to examine man's ontological concerns with impartiality, as if I were discussing another race of beings.

If what I articulate rings with a sense of authenticity, it derives from the reverberation in the reader of each of our struggles with the anguish and disillusionment of being in a world that we did not make, in which each of us was thrust as a disinherited Self.

The utility of the position I espouse in this volume I suspect cannot be appreciated without the reader's continual struggle, as he encounters my statements, with his own entrenched beliefs and core attitudes about how he must maintain himself-in-the-world. This struggle may not be one all readers are willing or should be encouraged to undergo at this time. This is a necessary caution. Whereas I have in this volume attempted to develop strategies for exploring the stances the Self projects onto the world and their underlying assumptions, at the same time I have tried to refrain from offering them as formulas of resolution of the narcissistic dilemmas that plague the Self's existence.

This volume is organized as follows: chapter one describes the requirements of a Self theory of action. Chapter two explores the narcissistic dilemma of modern man. Chapters three, four, and five are essays, both philosophical and empirical, which describe creative Self theory. Chapters six, seven, eight, and nine are clinical explorations of the dilemmas of modern man. Chapter six is also the author's statement of his own personal struggle with these ontological imperatives. Chapter ten, the concluding chapter, delineates a research project to more fully investigate the psychotherapeutic implications of the position espoused in this volume.

Chapter One

The Ethical Requirements of a Self Theory

"Like learned literary men, psychologists too speak of other men's emotions. But what of their passions . . . A description of someone else's emotion is one thing; understanding one's own is something else. And our problem is to understand, for *me (us)*, subjectively, what it is *to have* an emotion."

—Robert C. Solomon

We live in conflictive and distrustful times. The ordered society of yesteryear has dissipated, leaving behind eroded structures and clouds of cynicism and discontentment. We are immobilized by complex social problems that appear insoluble. We yearn for the warm regard and assurance of others. We want to touch others deeply and caringly, but instead draw back in fear of our own malevolence, no less than that of our neighbors. We impute that we are not responsible for the destructive actions we have accorded others. We have tried to act as best we can to survive and to survive with our integrity intact. Toward these efforts Alexander Solzhenitsyn, the defiant defender of human rights, has bitterly depicted the Western world as plagued by a loss of courage and a destructive and irresponsible freedom which has been granted without limitation. In a word, we live in an era in which men find it onerous to accept responsibility for their own actions and for the embittered and hollow course their existence has taken.

Who are the modern men to whom I am referring? Let us meet them! The mechanical Mickey Mouse: It walks; it talks; it mimics a human being; its headpiece is filled with small metallic gears—one for every emotion; each movement of the automaton accompanied by its extended arms, grasping blindly. Who will wind it? Who will set it on its way?

The nebbish: He has long felt alone; a loneliness that seems to have no object, a loneliness not merely born of physical confinement—but more an estrangement born of ignorance. He feels held by some internal force within a crowd of vague faces and stolid hearts—physically near, emphatically indifferent to his plight. He seeks to reach out, to extend himself—to but garnish at the smallest pittance of concern. And finds that he knows not how!

Each, the automaton and the nebbish, curses the cruel God that shaped him so strangely. Why was he marked so odd? Odd piece is he, with no counterpart to soothe him.

In a word, man's guidelines for living stand broken, disjointed, and in disarray. No longer do men have clear reasons for living and for endeavoring. To whatever modern man attends he discovers evidence that his presence is unnecessary. The magnitude and comprehensiveness of modern technology are such that a relatively few scientists and technicians can serve the physical requirements of the entire population. Modern man has been informed that God is dead; indeed, in man's ignorance and in his despair, he may have slain him. Nonetheless, he need not fear a dead God. Man finds that he is no longer held responsible for the children he has produced, nor the spouse to which he was once committed. Modern man's existence may be freely egocentric and asocial to a degree not tolerated but a short while past. He is not actually required, other than in terms of an antiquated moral sense, to maintain a trade and life style forged on supporting immediate and extended family. In the past, a man's destiny had always been his family. They were the root and essence of his existence. He could no more evade this commitment than obviate the realization that he had produced offspring who required his care and protection. Today, with the high rate of changing families through divorce and remarriage, a man may not be required by law to support the woman he took in matrimony, nor the children their union produced. If other people do not take up his financial and social responsibilities, there are public agencies designed to do precisely that (Goldberg, 1977[a]).

In a recent book Christopher Lasch (1978) argues that our Western society appears to have exhausted its supply of constructive ideas. We have become intellectually, morally, and dramatically bankrupt and uninventive. In its stead, according to Lasch:

> Capitalism has evolved a new political ideology, welfare liberalism which absolves individuals of moral responsibility and treats them as victims of social circumstances. It has evolved a new mode of social control, which deals with the deviant as a patient and substituted medical rehabilitation for punishment It has given rise to a new culture, the narcissistic culture of our time, which has translated the predatory individualism of the American

Adam into a therapeutic jargon that celebrates not so much individualism as solipsism, justifying self-absorption as "authenticity" and "awareness." [P. 218]

In support of Lasch's thesis we readily find that modern man has been persuasively defended from experiencing accountability for his acts of madness, destructiveness, and lack of consideration for his neighbors by psychiatry, the modern Pharisees. The "sickness–no responsibility model" was created by early psychoanalytic practitioners to free the guilt-immobilized client from feelings he could not acknowledge because of their forbidden nature. This moral recasting of untoward feelings contributed toward enabling persons of past decades to be more direct and congruent in their dealings with their fellows. However, the situation has now eroded to where psychological defenses have come to justify nonproductivity and antisocial behavior. "I don't relate well to people. I have a fear" has become an entrenched defense against commitment and community, resulting in an unending archaeological search for the reason for the victim's fears.

Every action has a reaction. No longer susceptible to external punishment, redistribution, or societal sanction for his actions, his guilt for his untoward acts lies ulcerous in modern man's gut. In short, modern man no longer is required to be involved and committed to other Selves and projects in the world. His protean defenders have dissuaded him from the pursuit of passion, companionship, social utility, and community endeavor, as they have ferreted out that these motives are actually epiphenomenological, products of unresolved oedipal and narcissistic strivings. Modern man finds himself footloose and uncentered by the unburdening of his commitments to an indifferent world.

These considerations suggest, as I seem intent on emphasizing as a major theme in each of my books, that the individual in American society has been set emotionally adrift by the dissolution of the traditional anchoring institutions of his social systems. In the past, these venerable ethical, social, and occupational concepts and beliefs of religious, family, and work-guild membership served to define the role and the function of each societal member. The individual who was able to internalize these societal concepts derived a sense of identity and value as a member of society. Today, our anchoring societal institutions are no longer able to absorb the intellectual and emotional energies of the denizen. The individual must define for himself his place in an ever-changing world. Morality is now regarded as situational, tentative, and open to revision. Public and private commitments are no longer absolutely binding as they were within the more ordered and less questioned societal guidelines.

The individual today is forced to question for himself the meaning of life: "Who am I?" "How did I get this way?" "Where shall I go?" The more the individual must rely upon his own resources for solving personal difficulties, the more he is in touch with feelings of self-denigration, frustration, and anguish. The individual today feels that he is ailing, possessed by a sickness that is neither physical nor simply emotional, but rather a malaise of spirit, a sickness of alienation,[1] the "Sickness of the Soul" so poignantly described by the philosophers William James and Soren Kierkegaard, derived from an uncommitted presence in the world, no less epidemic and socially contagious despite its absence of an organic etiology.

It has been contended that modern man's sickness of the soul is derived from his uneasiness rendered by his act of parricide. In slaying God he cast himself into a state of aloneness (see chapter two). Prior to this psychological event, man was never solitary. Cain first experienced aloneness by being abandoned by God upon the discovery of his fraticide. Today each of us is alone and has become increasingly more firmly entrenched in our solitary existence through our continual acts of silent fraticide.

The existential psychologist views the malaise of spirit of modern man as an ontological condition predicating all emotional and social disturbances, be they characterological or due to a brief situational crisis. Modern man seeks more than the perpetuation of his existence; he yearns for personal and transcendental meaning for his presence. Individuals possessed by ontological malaise frequently have attempted conventional forms of psychological treatment and other forms of remedial actions—meditation, EST, Esalen, and the like—languishing in these situations, more frequently than not, more frustrated and disillusioned than when they entered. Particularly in terms of conventional psychotherapy, many individuals have found that the treatment takes too long, is uninvolving, and does not provide enough give-and-take between client and therapist to encourage the client out of his alienation and characterological disillusionment (Goldberg, 1977[a]).

The newer forms of psychological amelioration have their own serious limitations. The more cautious seeker must eventually recoil at the grandiose propaganda and hard-sell fanaticism of most of the new therapies (Goldberg, 1973). It often appears that the guru is trying as desperately to convince himself of the efficacy of his particular brand of salvation, as he is of enabling the client to experience its utility. For all of these remedial endeavors, conventional, no less than radical approaches, there is too often an absence of a set of values and the lack of a meaningful code for conducting one's existence. Moreover, the actual motive inherent in our search for therapy often may be a malevolent one, as Peter Marin (1975) has so insightfully inferred. He argues that

> most of us realize at one level of consciousness or another that we inhabit an age of catastrophe—if not for ourselves then for countless others. Try as we do, we cannot ignore the routine inequities of consumption and distribution which benefit us and condemn others to misery. Each of us must feel a kind

of generalized shame, an unanswered sense of guilt. So we struggle mightily to convince ourselves that our privilege is earned or deserved, rather than [as we must often feel unconsciously] a form of murder or theft. Our therapies become a way of hiding from the world, a way of easing our troubled conscience.

In a word, modern man has yet to realize that self understanding without the presence of passion and concern disables him from forming a commitment to fully participate in the world. This persisting dilemma of modern man was revealed to me in a daydream of a patient. He entitled it "one's duty":

He heard the wild, ranting, shrieks of the wild, fanatic herd of the 'driven' masses. They cried for blood—red, rich, pure blood. He looked down upon his love—his beautiful meaning of existence lying pale and frightened on the bed. One idea filled his head—obliviating all else: 'one should do his duty.' He put one hand under her precious head of silken hair, and another under her petrified limbs. The hands that once trembled and shook were now poised and collected. Her face loomed up at him for one moment, a frightened, innocent question hovering upon her bloodless lips—it had become now a meaningless face!

"He pushed open the French windows and walked out on to the balcony. He raised his sacrifice above his head and dropped her into the ravenous clutches of the mass of assembled beasts. He, then, turned away from her ordeal—and, for a brief moment felt a flow of tranquility—he had done his duty. He had 'torn the heart out of his chest,' now he, too, could be a machine!"

The persistent, troubling dilemma of modern man contained in the dream above has proven resistive to psychotherapeutic efforts. Many practitioners have a difficult time reaching clients who appear to function adequately in their daily activities but who, at the same time, are detached from their surroundings and have minimal involvement with any other person and no firm commitment to any endeavor (Ruitenbeek, 1970). The narcissistic personality is well suited for the computer age in many respects. Lasch (1978) indicates that

> for all his inner suffering, the narcissist has many traits that make for success in bureaucratic institutions, which put a premium on the manipulation of interpersonal relations, discourage the formulation of deep personal attachments, and at the same time provide the narcissist with the approval he needs in order to validate his self-esteem. [Pp. 43–44]

Insofar as practitioners develop aversive reactions in their ephemeral struggles with these clients, psychotherapy proves to be counterproductive for persons afflicted with ontological malaise (Goldberg, 1977[a]).

Social Philosophy

As a book on values and social action, I am concerned in this volume with what man is, chooses to remain, and what he can become. As such, this volume is presented as social philosophy. Philosophy is a discipline of human knowledge that seeks to advance man's knowledge of himself and of the universe in which he dwells by critically examining and evaluating the nature of man's ideas and the influence these ideas have on his conduct and actions. However, philosophy in recent decades has become rather academic, professional, and as a result has distanced itself from the existential concerns of modern man's endeavor to live a more productive and meaningful life. This is unfortunate, for I believe that philosophy has a considerable contribution to make to not only examining ontological malaise but also to abetting modern man in creatively coming to terms with his human condition. Social philosophy, enriched with the realizations and insights from man's creative achievements in the arts may enable us to resurrect a more efficacious psychotherapy.

This endeavor will, however, be an onerous task. As a psychotherapist and psychotherapy educator, I am troubled by the disturbing realization that psychotherapy, certainly conventional psychotherapy, is in a state of serious crisis and that its future is in doubt. For many clients, perhaps for most, psychotherapy is not an answer, certainly not a total answer to alienation and disillusionment in their lives. What is my disenchantment with psychotherapy based on? I will address this issue in the following pages.

The Paucity of Meaningful Therapeutic Endeavor

Kierkegaard long ago indicated that the concepts of meaning and emotionality are inseparable human experiences. Meaningful experience of the Self can only come from a passionate commitment in concrete relation with other objects. Commitment alone is lonely and unrewarding, lacking energy. Passion by itself is aimless and quickly spent, lacking endurance. Attempts to analytically separate human meaning and emotionality have resulted from epistemological endeavors to understand human experience by formulating a scientific—by means of a deterministic—discipline and methodology. This endeavor has had an ironic effect on the way we view human behavior. It has extolled the observation of behavior while at the same time it has devalued the direct experience of existence. It is hardly curious, then, that the observer (for example the scientist or the practioner) is regarded as the expert of the other person's behavior, whereas the subject or the patient is regarded as naive or deluded in understanding the intent of his own behavior. Epistemological endeavors to understand human behavior as a deterministic system have, in short, resulted in a *Weltanschauung* in which there are experts and novices in understanding the nature and experience of objective and psychological realities, arguing that a knowledge of theory enables the psychologically trained observer to decipher objective reality, as well as to understand other Selves more perceptively than they know themselves.

As a psychotherapy educator, it is rather apparent to me that practitioners have unquestioningly, for the most part, acted as if this knowledge gives them the perdgative to steer other Selves away from what they purport to want, to what they actually need in terms of their psychological development (Goldberg, 1978[a]). Practitioners who regard themselves as experts about objective reality and their clients' subjective reality, discard consensus reality[2] as an operational definition of reality, in favor of wrestling away the "illusion" of reality from the client's idiosyncratic world and replacing this "illusion" with the therapist's world as reality.

Notwithstanding, empirical evidence defies the claims of any brand of psychotherapy that it is impressively cogent in understanding and treating emotional distress. "Mental illness" is one of the most serious problems facing the United States. It is estimated that one of every four hospital beds in the United States is occupied by a patient diagnosed as "schizophrenic." Moreover, several million persons consult psychotherapists each year. Few families lack a family member who is afflicted by some serious manifestation of emotional distress. There is considerable evidence that a large proportion of those who enter psychological treatment leave psychotherapy relatively unimproved, sometimes even after several years of treatment and large expenditures of emotional and financial investment. Mental health and psychotherapy services are not simply ineffective in a large number of instances, preventing troubled people from getting the psychological help they desperately need. Even more disturbing is the evidence (see Goldberg, 1977[a]) that practitioners who do not carefully concern themselves with the epistemological and ethical concerns raised in psychotherapy frequently exacerbate the difficulties their clients bring them.

In fairness to the psychotherapy professions, I must point out that mental health practice has not reached the maturity of a science. In the development of a science there is a need for a strategy of discovery, as well as a strategy of precision. In recent years psychologists and other social scientists, in whimsical deification of the precision of method and theory exhibited by the physical scientists, have exerted their efforts perhaps too exclusively in the development of precision tools. There has developed, as a consequence, in psychology a great advance in the theory and practice of measurement (Goldberg, 1970[a]). Unfortunately, the results of our elaborate measurements aren't worth a damn, until we know more about the variables we are supposed to be measuring. Before this can occur, practitioners must carefully address several important ethical and epistemological issues. A major issue I am concerned with in this volume is that of restoring a sense of purpose and meaningfulness to the clinical situations with which we daily are confronted by exploring some of the salient ontological conditions predicating the therapeutic encounter.

Psychotherapy as a Reductionistic System

Let us first examine some of the difficulties involved in exploring the ontological conditions inherent in the therapeutic situation. Whereas religious teachings and moral philosophy were utilized to set standards of socially acceptable conduct in the past, now what is regarded as "psychologically healthy" attitudes and practices have been substituted (Goldberg, 1977[a]). At one time psychotherapy was a specialized medical technique for only a narrow and circumscribed patient population; it is now considered to be the *sine qua non* application in all matters in which human suffering is involved (Small, 1971). The craft of psychotherapy is now expected to provide answers to questions about malfunction in all areas of human endeavor. The twentieth century has awakened to a fervent exploration of man's psyche in all its irrational depths. The reader need only glance at current periodicals or view cinema or television dramas to readily appreciate that most complex human problems and concerns are typically reduced to the level of psychological explanation. The ideas of Sigmund Freud and his followers, although they may seem somewhat less impressive than they were two decades past, nevertheless remain as influential in modern living and thought as the ideas of any personality who has lived in the last century. The questions are, of course, "Is this influence justified?" and "What are the implications of psychological reductionism and explanation?"

I strongly believe that the reduction of man's life, his interests, his interactions, his motives, and his sentiments has diverted modern man from the directness and immediacy of his experiences. It has left modern man a ponderous, introspective reactor and, at the same time, deprived him of skills in engaging openly and directly with others. A prime example of this is the discouragement of guilt feelings by modern psychotherapy. It well can be argued that a sense of guilt should not be discouraged. The experience of guilt means that the Self is involved in a significant avoidance of its commitment to deal with a relationship, a project, or a sentiment which the Self holds in value. On the other hand, once the Self takes responsibility for its abnegation of its values, it is no longer in avoidance, its presence is confirmed, and the Self relinquishes its sense of guilt. Psychiatry has destructively freed modern man from this vital imperative in man's quest for meaning.

It is unfortunate that the methods of psychological inquiry which once sought to free man from the bonds of his repressed motives have come full circle, rendering modern man a prisoner of his own introspective search. The psychological man is less concerned with what he is directly experiencing with others, as with what he infers or seeks to find is the "real" reason or motive behind why people treat him as they do. A kiss that should taste delectably sweet is denied its flavor, a caress its tender touch, a smile its assurance—for the recipient is continually exposed to psychological propaganda that maintains that all emotions mask transferential feelings from another face, another place, and another time.

Even as psychotherapies, in and of themselves, traditional and current methodologies, are partial and incomplete systems for ethical inquiry and growthful exploration of the human condition. These psychological systems are reactive, curative, and restorative. As such they are fashioned only to deal with ruptures in the individual's relationship with the existing order, not with the requirements of holistic growth and intentionality. David Shainberg (1978), a psychoanalyst who has closely studied Eastern thought, has written:

> "... there is something wrong about the way we think in psychiatry, where all our theories deal with fragmentation and the relationship between fragments. It is our lack of understanding of the holistic action of life that gives birth to this fragmentation.

I trust that the reader is not waiting for me to finally unwrap the banner of therapeutic truth and invincibility after I HAVE INVALIDATED THE OTHER schools of psychotherapy. I hold no therapeutic truths up my sleeve. Fragmentation of approach is true of the existential position to which I identify, as with other psychotherapies, despite the attention given by existentialists to man as a holistic being in their writings. The existential approach in psychotherapy, as with other ontological approaches has, according to Elkin

> failed to give rise to an adequate depth psychology, one that resolves the "existential dilemma" of freedom-unfreedom that besets any quest for a sense of more truly personal identity. For authenticity and freedom are in themselves, strictly speaking, manifest only in the power of negation (Erich Fromm's "Freedom from"). Devoid of positive content, these concepts cannot provide an ethic for responsible human action. That is why existential unmasking, from Nietzsche on, has often led to cynicism and despair....
> [1977]

What psychotherapy has lacked is a guide for living that has evolved from the therapeutic struggle to come to terms with the human condition. This guide cannot be simply exhortative or simplistic and insulting. It is, therefore, for example, unlike the methods of Ellis (1962) and Glasser (1965). It must do justice to the complexity of the human dilemma and is therefore, for example, unlike Maslow (1962) and humanistic therapists such as Schutz (1971). It must be a guide which, while focusing on a continual struggle for creating enlightenment and meaning for the individual, does not lose the integrity of the individual as a unique Self in mass cathexis to social and political movements—therefore, for example, unlike Fromm (1963).

A Philosophical Position must be Functional

Having a relatively pragmatic orientation to the concerns of human existence, I view as extravagant philosophical positions that are not addressed to guidelines to enable man to act enlightenedly in his ontological struggle. I hold, as did Nietzsche: one should experiment with all so-called truths. Every truth needs be confronted with the question: "Can I live it?" Men do not choose whether or not they hold a philosophy of life. Rather, man's experience with his human condition necessitates his having to take a particular point of view and interpretation of the nature of the universe in which he exists—as Rational-Emotive psychotherapy and the Objectivist School of Philosophy have argued. But man does choose whether or not this interpretation is conscious or unconscious, rational or irrational, functional or dysfunctional.

My professional training has been as a clinician and psychotherapist, rather than as a philosopher.[3] I recognize psychotherapy, however, to be a designed and applied manifestation of social philosophy. I believe that, despite many serious epistemological, moral, and practical limitations in the theory and practice of psychotherapy, it has something to offer us as a social philosophy. I will endeavor in this volume to examine psychotherapy, as the human arena in which I am most knowledgeable, as well as literature and the arts as expressions of social philosophy intended to enable modern man to live as best he can the good life. However, although I will devote several chapters to certain issues in psychotherapy and explore what psychodynamic examination can bring to bear on the narcissistic dilemmas of the Self and its relation to other Selves, this is not a book on psychotherapeutic treatment or methodology. It is, however, a companion volume to a book I am currently writing called "Masters of the Therapeutic Arts" (see chapter ten for a detailed discussion of this project).

A Defense of Narcissism

As I have reiterated, after many years of practice as a psychologist and as a psychotherapist, I have come to recognize certain limitations in psychological theory that mitigate against enabling me and those with whom I have worked to meaningfully and creatively fulfill our human potential. Clinical discussion of narcissism is an example of this. Narcissistic affliction has come in recent years to be imputed as a clinical entity at work in every resistive and difficult clinical manifestation and every untoward societal event.

The concept of narcissism is derived from Ovid's myth of Narcissus, a beautiful youth who rejected the interests of his admirers until one day the Gods, in angry reaction to his assuming the Gods' prerogative of pride and indifference, caused him to fall in love with his own reflection in a pool of water. Narcissus fell in love with his own reflection with such abandonment that he gazed transfixed upon it until he wasted away. According to Garfield Tourney:

> The initial introduction of the term [Narcissism as a] psychological phenomena was made by Ellis in 1898; he described a special state of auto-erotism as Narcissus-like. In this condition the sexual emotions become absorbed or entirely lost in self-admiration. The normal germ of narcissism was regarded as particularly significant in women. Contemporary with Ellis, the German psychiatrist Näcke, who referred to the work of Ellis, used the term "narcismis" simply as a translation of Ellis' "Narcissus-like tendency" in speaking of extreme self-admiration as a special variant of auto-erotism.
>
> Freud and the psychoanalysts made the decisive introduction of the concept of narcissism into their theories. In his first edition (1905) of *Three Contributions to the Theory of Sexuality,* Freud wrote of auto-erotism but not of narcissism; the concept of narcissism was introduced into this work after he completed his paper "On Narcissism" in 1914. Having derived the term from Näcke and Ellis, Freud spoke of narcissism as a sexual perversion in which one's body is taken as a sexual object. Freud also conceptualized narcissism in a broader sense to include the libidinal component of the instinct of self-preservation. Narcissism became incorporated into Freud's libido theory as an initial phase, primary narcissism, in which the individual is unaware of sources of pleasure outside the Self and attaches to himself or herself a degree of omnipotence. Eventually the ego attaches itself to objects, mainly parents, who become the source of gratification. However, the longing for a state of narcissism remains. Freud used the concept of narcissism to explain many psychotic phenomena. He also distinguished a narcissistic character formation which probably has been more readily incorporated into psychiatric nomenclature than all other concepts of narcissism. [1978]

In contemporary usage, narcissism has been defined psychodynamically as the investment and refusal to give up fixed conceptions of the world in face of dissonant information—particularly, how the Self needs to relate to others and how the Self must be treated by them. We are told that narcissistic personalities lack empathy with others, finding it difficult to enter into close relationships, are self-centered, and have an insatiable need for admiration. They regard others as existing only as a means for obtaining his or her desires. Furthermore, we are told narcissistic persons depend upon the vicarious warmth provided by others, while concomitantly fearing their dependency on others. They experience a sense of inner emptiness, boundless repressed rage, and insatiable oral cravings, and such secondary characteristics as pseudo-self-insight, calculating seductiveness, and self-deprecating humor. Some analysts such as Otto Kernberg (1978) argue that it is self-hatred, rather than self-love, that lies at the root of pathological narcissism. According to Kernberg:

> . . . Self-hatred is more dominant in the narcissist than is self-love. Narcissists have very low opinions of themselves and this is why they constantly seek approbation. They consider themselves unworthy and unloveable, and seek constantly to hide this fact from themselves by trying to get the outside world to proclaim them unique, extraordinary, great. But beyond that they suffer from intense, unconscious envy that makes them want to spoil, deprecate and degrade what others have and they lack, particularly others' capacity to give and receive love.

I differ from the negative view portraying narcissism described above. I feel that the attacks on certain manifestations of narcissism have prevented us from removing the Pandora lid of narcissism to fully understand the concept and its useful and creative implications. Like Kohut (1977) I have come to view narcissism not as a pejorative concept, but rather as the mainspring of the struggle for human creativity and meaningful human exploration. Also like Kohut, I view healthy narcissism as enhancing to the fulfillment of human existence as narcissistic disturbances are deleterious to the Self's ability to function maximally and with a sense of gratification and enrichment. Narcissism, as Kohut points out, is misunderstood if it is regarded simply as a temporary phase of psychosexual development to be mitigated in order to be replaced by mature object love. Narcissistic strivings coexist with mature object love, both confounding and enriching its development.

In my view, central dynamics in understanding creative endeavors, as well as dysfunctional narcissism, are those of fortitude and stubbornness. The creative endeavor of the Self comes about in the Self's refusal to give up inspired ideas, passionate concerns, and rebellious stances toward the social order until they have been enacted in meaningful endeavor. Narcissism, in its positive sense, is the unwillingness to be dissuaded, discouraged, or ridiculed against giving birth to the most audacious and grandiose projects. It is a commitment to passion as an enrichment of human experience. The hallmark of narcissism is the refusal to let others' rationality dissuade passion from its rightful place as a torchbearer in an indifferent and stolid universe. (See chapters four and five for a discussion of this notion).

Moreover, the importance of narcissism resides in the fact that reality—or at least the reality with which we have the means to master—is invented (see Chapter five). There is, then, a need for creative self-investment in the world. By believing and valuing its inventions—by commitment to a perspective or a way of being—and communicating the value of its inventions to others, the Self creates a reality in which an ensemble of Selves can come together to share, encounter, and meaningfully experience together the world.

In sum, the theory of personality offered in this volume views the Self as the core of personality rather than as a manifestation or epiphenomenon derived from the struggle between unconscious, intrapsychic tensions and environmental forces. This is aimed at examining psychological and philosophical epistemological notions about the nature of the Self. In this volume I have attempted to dispel the notion that personality can be defined and understood in terms of what it "is" (an essentialistic position), rather than what the Self does. What the Self does defines itself. There is nothing beyond the nature of the act as the intention of the Self. Personality consists of the composite of specific acts the Self takes toward other Selves and events, and the value and the meaning the Self imbues these objects in regard to these acts. Concerns about the personality of the Self can only be meaningfully explored within the context of the interaction of the Self and its intended objects. How can the Self find meaning other than in meaningful encounter with other Selves, in which the Self is able to articulate and negotiate for values (the Self's intentions) with others? Personal identity is only meaningful in terms of other Selves. There is no need to have an identity simply in terms of relation to one's Self.

A system of personality would be of little function as a guide for living unless the Self could take purposive action. The theory of Self to be described in this volume emphasizes the importance of human will in behavior (see chapter four). This theory also recognizes that purposive human action depends both on freedom, as well as it does on a natural order of events. I have given considerable attention to demonstrating the compatibility of "freedom" and "determinism" (see chapters four and five). Moreover, as a system of growth and enlightenment, the relation between these constructs must advisably be imbued with—or make possible—the articulation of desirable human character, such as courage and commitment. This is described in chapter five.

The theory of personality described in this volume has serious implications for the practice of psychotherapy (see Chapter nine). Psychotherapy that "frees" the Self from reference to other Selves and reference groups, no matter how exploitive and constricting they may have been, casts the Self into a value vacuum.[4] Several practitioners have been aware of this dilemma. Nonetheless, they have tried to avoid exploring values and have instead taught techniques, for example "learning to fight fairly" or to "think rationally" and so forth, rather than helping their clients develop a frame of reference based upon their existential concerns and struggles.

It is true that I break tradition with the existing theories of personality with which I have been taught as a graduate student and trained with as a clinician. Of course my ideas about Selfhood did not spring from a vacuum or entirely from my own personal speculation and experience. These ideas have in large part issued from my exploration of existential and phenomenological philosophy and the recent writing of Robert C. Solomon (1977) on the nature of the passions.

Chapter Two

The Saga of Don Juan Retold—Rebellion and the Narcissistic Dilemma

O gentle child, beautiful as thou wert, why didst thou leave the trodden paths of men too soon, and with weak hands though mighty heart dare the unpastured dragon in his den?

—Percy B. Shelley

The poet laments:[1]

I weep for Adonais—he is dead!
Oh, weep for Adonais! though our tears
Thaw not the frost which binds so dear a head!

The poet exhorts further:[2]

Oh, weep for Adonais—he is dead!
Wake, melancholy mother, wake and weep!
Yet wherefore? Quench within their burning bed
Thy fiery tears, and let thy loud heart keep
Like his, a mute and uncomplaining sleep;

Why does she not weep? Why does she not awaken? Perhaps she cannot weep for a son she has long ago abandoned! And where is your father, Adonais? Why is he not here to mourn you? Obviously, a slain father will not return to mourn his assassin! Who is this disturbing Adonais? Do we know him? Know him we should! Adonais, referred to by different names, is found in legend in every land. Best known, no doubt, is the Don Juan saga by Tirso de Molina.[3]

The following chapter depicting the character of Don Juan is an endeavor to examine psychologically through poetic revelation and folk legend the struggles of the man who attempts to combine passion and sensitivity with his keen intellect, in seeking personal meaning in a world in which he finds no firm values and is confronted with tentative and hypocritical codes of morality—systems that he finds readily accessible to manipulation and loose interpretation.

What we first need take cognizance of in examining the character of Don Juan is his sentiment that each of his progenitors in their respective ways has failed him. His relationship to his father was intellectual and distant. It may well be referred to as "cosmic disillusionment." The reader cannot be certain whether Juan is resentful toward his mortal father or whether he is referring to the deity purported to have created the world. His relationship to his mother is more personal and ambivalent. Juan feels impaired by her. He was led to believe that all he had to do was smile. The message, however, was bereft of conviction. After all, what did she know, everything else she told him was invalid!

Emotionally, then, Don Juan feels excluded from exemplary role-modeling and parental guidance. He is compelled, without his conscious realization, to invent himself and to create a world in which to address his tormented longings and fervent ambitions. The reader might well ask if Don Juan is mad. He well may be! But clearly his inventions are successful, in that he is able to seduce women and cajole men into accepting even his most outrageous inventions as "desirable."

We would today call Don Juan a narcissistic character.[4] The character we are examining, however, is not simply a man who has lived in a single age. Ortega y Gassett (1969) points out that Don Juan may mean two different things. Don Juan as a legend described in books, poems, and operas, and the character of Don Juan manifested in men throughout the ages. I am concerned, essentially, with the latter. Don Juan, then, is a character who has lived often before, lives today, and will live again, after all our neat psychological theories and reductionistic endeavors have been rejected and forgotten. Theories will not help us understand Don Juan's struggles. Otto Rank (Winter, 1975) understood this in part when he indicated that Mozart's opera about the Don Juan legend could not be logically understood in terms of psychological theory because the legend represents

> a revolutionary change which cannot be genetically traced from the individual's complexes, but can only be made intelligible through the understanding of the historical development of folk-tradition. [P. 31]

I would add to Rank's statement that we can best try to understand Don Juan from the reverberation of his hurt and disillusionment in our own struggles and our own silent longings to love and be loved in a cynical world.

Narcissism as a Moral Question

George Bernard Shaw, in the famous third act of *Man and Superman*[5] suggests that the narcissistic issue that pursues Don Juan is the moral question raised by Mozart in his opera:

> Does the man who possesses superb gifts—looks, charm, wealth, intellect and vitality—have the right to live for himself?

In Shaw's play the Devil emphatically exhorts Juan that he is entitled to utilize his gifts as he wishes. He argues that only through the life of the senses can man successfully avoid cynicism and despair in a world bereft of justice and empathetic concern for one's fellow man. In opposition, Donna Anna, a woman whom Don Juan has wronged, resulting in his stay in Hell, seeks to enlist Juan's assistance in what she (and, apparently, G. B. Shaw) claims are Don Juan's moral prerequisites—to produce and rear the best in the human species, a superman.

Shaw's Don Juan is persuaded by neither the Devil's nor Donna Anna's options. In fact, he appears to prefer a retreat from human company where he can pursue his philosophical speculations without the distraction of others' wishes and demands. In perhaps all the other interpretations of the legend, Don Juan readily accepts the Devil's guidance. According to Winter (1975), Don Juan's identification with the Devil is a defense against the threat Donna Anna represents. In identifying with purely materialistic and instinctual values, Don Juan

> acts out a fear of losing his mortal soul through marriage and children. . . . [P. 31]

His rebellion against spiritual values casts Don Juan as a protagonist of modern man. Other protagonists in literature before the legend of Don Juan have, for the most part, responded to Don Juan's dilemma with a sheer inability to escape their responsibilities to others to use their gifts in an accountable manner. But their authors, it seems to me, have had essentially political or moralistic rather than existential concerns in resolving their protagonists' dilemmas. This was certainly true of Shakespeare and of the ancient Greek dramatists. Even more recently, Tennyson, for example, responds to Homer's political figure, Odysseus, and warns us of Odysessus's accountability for his gifts. Odysseus, we were told by Homer, wished to live out his life quietly with his beautiful and faithful wife, Penelope. Because of his extraordinary gifts of cleverness and statesmanship, he is morally required to respond to the exigencies facing the Greek nations to lead them away from the pending supplication to their enemies. Twenty years of his prime of manhood are spent in political endeavors apart from his family and homeland. Odysseus cannot avert his moral journey, Tennyson tells us:

> It little profits an idle king,
> I cannot rest from travel: I will drink
> Life to lees: all times I have enjoyed
> Greatly, have suffered greatly, both with those
> That love me, and alone,...
> How dull it is to pause, to make an end,
> To rust unburnished, not to shine in use!
> As though to breathe were life...

Don Juan—The Misunderstood Protagonist

At first glance the consequences for Don Juan's egotistic pursuits seem obvious. Don Juan must suffer for not submitting himself to the moral solution taken by other protagonists, such as Odysseus, who examine and vivify their lives responsibly. In whatever form in literature or opera the legendary figure Don Juan appears, he suffers severely from self-indulgence. His refusal to participate and commit himself to any project, save his lusts and his occupation as a dilettante of the senses, earns him the ultimate retribution of damnation and hell.

But matters run deeply, we suspect, with this much maligned and misunderstood figure when we hear him cry out:

> Who has driven the light out of my world? What has happened to the warm, protected and rejoicing days promised to me in my youth—the summers of pride—if I chose the virtuous life? They have vanished like lost sands into a starless night! I live in a world in which I am a stranger, a world which I do not know. I seek to find in intimacy with a woman that from which I have always felt excluded. I seek to return to innocence so that I might taste the fruits that seemed once so much the promise of my world and which are impossible to obtain alone. I return from my amorous encounters disillusioned. I cannot return to innocence. I know cynically too much. I am too aware of the price that I would have to pay for the promised

fruits of my youth. I am too imbued with the compromises I must undergo in each encounter to taste fresh the fruit. And, yet, I must continue my quest. Who has driven the light out of my world?

We are puzzled by Juan's sad canto. Don Juan has all the desired personal attributes. Why is he not content? Why does he long for a dead world, lost pursuits, and childhood promises he claims never fulfilled when all he need do is to ask any woman for whatever he desires and she will be his? As in response to our questions, we hear Juan exclaim:

> And the muses bequested that I shall have all things save one—choose! And I fallaciously assumed that to have all gifts, then self-esteem would inexorably ensue. How surreptitiously blinded was I, to have all gifts save self-esteem is to flaunt all, to enjoy none!

What does Juan mean by this curious statement? This is not the Don Juan we ostensibly know from legend.

Don Juan, the Trepid Hero

The contention has always been that Don Juan is a phallic character—an exhibitionist who acts out his narcissistic disturbance in order to avoid painful introspection, and because he has been unwilling to rationally digest the absurdity of the figure he casts. We are told that Don Juan has been shaped by his upbringing to believe that he can charm any woman, impress or intimidate any man. The Don Juan of legend is eternally optimistic. For him the perfect woman is always just around the corner, he has only to search a while longer.

No, this is not the Don Juan that presents himself to us. The character we see before us is beset with agitated trepidation.[6] Don Juan has been called many contemptible names, but what is most true of him is that he is frightened of his alleged gifts. His compulsive attempts to conquer women are his repeated efforts to reassure himself. We hear Juan exclaim:

> Many women have I known. Many loves have I. Notwithstanding, I am drawn to the woman who slights me, who refuses my seductive ways. What does she know that other women do not see or will not heed? If only I can charm her perhaps I can rid myself of my burning doubts!

His fears inform all things that constitute Don Juan. These fears have no name—they are unfathomable, unable to be evaded, and without mitigation. They can be momentarily outrun, never finally escaped.

In examining Don Juan we experience a character who has learned that significant others in his life are undependable in guiding his existence and, most particularly, in their emotional availability to him. Juan is always in a hurry in his passionate coming-togethers. He must prove his manhood, and it is for this that he compulsively goes on and on in his conquests. This is, of course, the phallic element in the saga of Don Juan, but it is the disturbed, oral qualities of his quest that most interest us.

The Search for the "Reparative Mother"

Juan tires of the monotony of his successes. He claims that any pursuit worth obsessing about isn't worth doing. Instead of joy, he sulks, he feels resentful. Don Juan wants a constant companion. He gets tired of always having to be Don Juan—always having to be prepared for a new adventure. He would like to let his guard down, to reveal his soul openly and completely. The stranger Juan seeks to encounter is his own shadow, the soul mate to his own soul. Juan's cynicism covers his deep hurt and his desperate desire to find a woman who is willing to journey with him as an equal—a partner who will engage him, confront him, and enable him to face up to the responsibilities of a meaningful relationship. He has found it painful that no woman can be his friend without trying to possess him. Women who say that they will accept his friendship alone, without possession, lash out at him for denying them his exclusive love, for his concerns about other women and for his doubts about himself.

Yet, Juan realizes that he needs perpetual confirmation. No matter what his previous conquests have been, or the lovely woman he has just left, when he is without a woman and sees another man with a woman, he feels that he is worthless and abject. Juan in childhood had been deprived of the security of quiet assurance and a sense of well-being. He feels resentful of having been thrust into a world in which he has been told that he need only smile; he has forged his life on this message and has found it finally to be vacuous. His mothering had been one of staccato upheavals and persistent anxiety. His mother's milk had been sour and unsettling. He never felt safe, quietly cared for, nor secure in the dependability of his surroundings. He was continually told "Keep busy—impress others, be nice, leave them liking you!" Concomitantly, Juan was given the metasense by his mother that no one—especially in authority—is to be truly trusted.[7] He has been told that it is vital to be cared for, but that this caring cannot be trusted.

The struggle for Don Juan has always been the pull to "lose Self," to become absorbed completely in the other and the extremely accentuated sense of Self—"Self-consciousness, the embarrassment of standing out." He feels hopeful only in the moments of sexual and erotic elation or in moments of amusement at his paradoxical and lamentable concern over his struggle to make some sense of his life. It is only in the sense that nothing matters or that everything matters that Don Juan feels alive. He cries out at other times: "I cared so much—that it doesn't matter!"

The caring that Juan struggles with cannot be meaningfully separated from his sexual presence. At such times as Don Juan's sexual prowess begins to diminish, he discovers that his sexual dissipation emanates from his deep despair and disappointment in not discovering "the reparative mother." Juan is on a perpetual quest to find the "enabling-reparative mother" whose touch and emotional intelligence will finally rid him of the confines of and the sense of having been issued from "the damaging mother." He finds, sadly, redemption in no woman. Since Juan cannot trust adoration, each woman he seduces loses her value to him shortly after she begins to adore him. Having received confirmation by a woman from her adoration, the adoration becomes untrustworthy. Juan loses interest in the woman and feels compelled to continue on his quest for the reparative mother. In a word, Don Juan is a man, Rank tells us (Taft, 1958), who seeks the ideal woman and cannot find her.

Narcissistic Pessimism

Don Juan of legend is seen as a libertine. We should realize at this point in our examination of Don Juan that his romanticism is pessimistic. We sense that in his lamenting musings as he lies by the side of a paramour:

> We lie side by side. You in your world. I in mine. Can I know your world? Can you know mine? Can I enter your world? Can you enter mine?

Don Juan has been told that love is the highest good. Haven't we been similarly told! Can we so easily ignore what W. H. Auden[8] wrote was "the error bred in the bone..."

> Of each woman and each man
> Craves what it cannot have
> Not universal love
> But to be loved alone.

Is it that Don Juan falls in love so easily or that he tries so hard to love that he cannot? Counter to the dictates of his cynical intellect, his desperate longing for the caring and contentment of secure love forces him to pursue women, only to find each time that the courtship leaves him feeling bitter and empty. His amorous adventures result in a life of fleeting relationships—the result of clever but disgraceful schemes. Nevertheless, they also evoke an exhilaration that is the only antidote he has fashioned to mitigate against his prolonged and intensive philosophical depression.[9] Don Juan finds that in moments of utter despair and disillusionment, only manic bursts of energy, ventures of dazzling seduction and intrigue avert the suicidal intensity of his despair and disillusionment. Without a woman Don Juan begins to lose the sense of being alive. He dare not reveal this fear. As a result, like Pirandello[10] characters who need the stage manager to continue to exist, he tells each woman he encounters that he wishes to live "only for a moment in you!"

Asked by each woman why he pursues her, Juan resorts to poetry to hide his fears. "What can I tell you!" exclaims Juan:

> Pure beauty is a wonderous jewel. It is a joy forever. It forces the sunset to return to its lair. I live for the moment when I behold my beloved. I live for no other moment as when I embrace my love. I become alive only when I become one with my other. When I enter her no other circumstances have any merit. I live forever in the arms and the eternity of my love.

Don Juan as a Romantic Protagonist

Don Juan's disillusionment comes from a basic honesty he expects from women and that he insists he is willing to return, but sadly finds missing in his amorous encounters. He is disillusioned that women so easily accept his cavalier ways, but are unwilling and unable to understand him. He points out:

> We are all strangers in the nights of our aloneness. Despite all efforts to love passionately and sincerely, despite our endeavors to realize our commitments to care for the other for himself you say to me, "I will love you always!"—knowing full well that to love me always is merely to lack another flame to light your candle. You say to me more reasonably, "I will keep in touch!" But, then, I know that your accounting letters reflect more the emptiness of your existence than any continuing ardor for me. You say to me most fairly, "I'll never forget you!" I realize, however, that better times absorb previous contentments.

Don Juan's cynicism and manipulation of relationships come from his eventual acclimation to the realization that only fools believe in universal justice; the man of wisdom and courage creates his own justice. Don Juan's charisma with women resides in his consummate willingness to promise the full moment of the present.

The poet[11] tells us that

> To a man love is a thing apart;
> To a woman it is her whole existence.

Don Juan was appreciated by women, for, like them, love was for Don Juan everything. This is reflected in a poem he often recited to his ladies:

> Is it not the heart that counts!
> Oh, that my heart were worthy of such sorrow,
> To have loved and lost thee,
> To have beheld paradise but briefly!
> Is it not the heart that counts!
> What if the pain must mount!
> Must the heart remain constant?
> Cannot brevity be its own essence?
> Does estrangement of being come of lack of physical actualization
> Or is it a heart too choked with fear for utterance?
> Heart, heart, bleating heart—call out!
> Let not the stolid world seal so soon my tomb!

Thus, while Don Juan gave each woman he was enticed by the full moment of his body and his soul, he was never able to avert his cynicism. The Spanish philosopher Ortega y Gassett (1969) helps us understand this when he indicates:

> Don Juan's vice is not, as a plebian psychologist assumes, fruitless sensuality. On the contrary, historical figures who, by their traits have contributed to the ideal character of Don Juan, were distinguished by an abnormal frigidity toward sexual pleasures. Don Juan's crime is in complelling woman after woman to "open up" in that miraculous scene, that pathetic instant in which the larva, in honor of a man, turns to a butterfly. When the scene is ended, the cold grimace returns to Don Juan's lips and, leaving the butterfly to burn her newly spread wings in the sun, he turns toward another Chrysalis. [P. 137]

Juan's suspicions about the unreliability of women have made him cynical. They have also rendered him a cautious man. His care is calculated in terms of the investment of his intensity. He constantly asks himself if he is choosing correctly. If he is wisely investing his energy and regard for a particular woman, would a better choice come around the corner a moment or two later? Should he hold back an instant longer? But if he tarries an instant too long, has he lost the propitious moment?

To avoid re-experiencing the "damaging mother," Juan waits for an invitation from whatever woman with whom he has become enticed. It might be a quiet smile, a fleeting glance that lingers an instant beyond the casual, and other most subtle cues. Ah, but the very instant after this signal, Juan in a flash is in stride, courting and charming his prey. Juan is schooled in the avoidance of initial rejection but secretly relishes the initial resistance of a woman to his ardent schemes. So he cynically informs them:

> See, there are no cards up my sleeve.
> What you see is what you get. If you don't like what you see, then, don't invite me into your heart. Above all, don't read into me and expect to get what I will not give!

Sadly, Juan knows that each prey will soon succumb to his intrigues, and within that knowledge resides his anguish and disappointment. For his schemes nauseate him. They reek of the mistrust he associates with the advice given to him by his damaging mother in facing the world: "Just smile and be friendly and all will be yours!"

If all enterprises are Juan's for only a smile, then nothing in particular is worth coveting, and there are no relationships that require commitment.

We must, however, realize that it is really Juan who is fooled by his own schemes. The personal pathos of Juan's schemes has not escaped all observers. Ortega y Gassett (1969) makes his major contribution to our understanding of Don Juan when he wisely points out:

> Don Juan is not the man who makes love to women, but the man whom women make love. [P. 27]

Don Juan is the perpetual child that women desire to mother. Juan contributes to his own self-deception by denying the realization that he breaks off his love affairs in order to injure these surrogate mothers in transferential revenge for the genuine love denied him by his own mother. Don Juan flees those women who touch him deeply. Juan fears being betrayed again as he was by his damaging mother. The notion of being betrayed or fooled by women is significant in the saga of Don Juan. His critics fail to see this; they focus rather on his phallic betrayal of women. Rank, according to Winter (1975)

> argues that the hostility of women toward Don Juan in the earliest versions of the legend is derived from the primal struggle to subdue the mother, who emerged as dominant after the slaying of the primal father. She protected the hero in order to use him as the instrument of her liberation; yet, on the other hand, she feels animosity toward him because he is an inadequate replacement for the slain father. [P. 22]

The poet[12] has forewarned us that Juan must repeatedly re-experience the interface of longing and disappointment. As much as Don Juan seeks the reparative mother, he fears and resents her, so he must destroy her. Thus, what the poet told Narcissus, so he speaks to Don Juan:

> What you seek is for nothing,
> What you love, you will destroy.

Don Juan as a Modern Protagonist

In addition to his sundry other crimes, Don Juan reeks of the curse of parricide. We hear him cry:

> Cursed be me, cursed be my name; for I am condemned to hell for a sin I do not experience, condemned to hell for a crime of which I had no physical involvement! I did not sin against God. It was He who fell from grace. It was for His original sin that I and every man am condemned. I have been driven out of Eden. He wished to deny me knowledge. Did He not understand that without the ability to live the examined life how can I learn why I act as I do? How can I choose those paths that best avert the clutches of everlasting death? For in forbidding me the chance to learn the fact and circumstances of my existence, God is dead. God exists because I am. In disbelieving in Him I denied Him His existence. This filled Him with shame. I have killed God. However, the penalty for parricide is to have to resurrect God within my own soul. I must become a more respectful, a more honest and, unfortunately, a more competent God than I have ever witnessed or have ever known. I have no recourse. I must become God simply to go on living as a mortal. I languish because I carry a corpse on my soul!

If we truly appreciate Juan's curse, we will see that as his own deity, his saga is Don Juan's vocation. He is restless, he feels out of sorts, at loose ends, without substance or purpose when he is not trying to justify his existence.[13] What is the justification of Don Juan's existence? We will examine this in the next section.

Narcissism, the Pursuit of Uniqueness

Given the folly of his pursuits, we ask if Juan must continue his struggle. Despite the painful compulsion of his struggles, he paradoxically responds:

The struggle that I feel forced to maintain enables me to see the world as few other men do.

We are puzzled by his statement. We simply want to know why Juan can't be happy. Why can't he be like other men? Why can't Juan fall in love and be content like any other man? Why does he think and feel and act in such extremes? He tells us that his uneasiness emanates from his prime foundation.

I have questioned the very ground on which I stand. This casts me without foundation in a bottomless abyss of uncertainty. I am forced intermittently to seize some foothold to break my fall into oblivion. The anchorages I seize are frequently more foolish and less firm foundations than those from which I cast myself. Yet not to pursue my quest is to deny my unique and special meaning to my existence.

Juan goes on to tell us that he feels as if he is held within the inescapable grips of constant self-doubts. This is the prison of his stubborness and his trepidation. This is the connection to his tragic flaw—to have all charms, save one, self-esteem.

Juan asks us: "Would you have me relinquish my longings, my reason for being?"

We finally realize the source of Juan's desperation. "No," we answer, "the world asks too much of you! For it asks nothing of you. It only asks that you be like all other men, undifferentiated emotionally; unique only in material possessions—objects of no moment."

Juan seems animated by our finally apprehending his struggle. He exclaims:

I am not of this earth, or this time. I awoke to the stillness of my rebirth. I am spun of different cloth. I march to a different drum. I am *un hombre de la mancha.* I have an impossible dream. As much as I purport my struggles as a reflection of the struggles of every man—the common man—it is my innermost need to seek and to be treated as unique, even if more flawed, more marred and in more anguish than other men, that gives me a sense of identity, the scepter of meaning.

Juan is telling us that he cannot calmly indulge himself in anything without the struggle to know if he deserves to feel that way. Don Juan quotes to us the canto of the narcissist: "Each man must do his thing or die!"

Don Juan saw in the streets of Sevilla a drunken peasant with empty sacks and wine bottles tapping out a flamenco beat in the middle of the cobblestone street, bent over and vulnerable to being struck by any moving vehicle. Similarly, Don Juan must retain his specialness. He can grant himself no rest from his quest. Without his narcissistic identity, Juan feels that he has no purpose, no reason for being. He secretly fears being uncovered as a fraud—found out to be only an ordinary man—no better, no worse than other men. Without specialness he experiences himself as worthless.

Truth as Persuasion

Don Juan's fervent need to be special has led to his being seen as an impostor and a manipulator. Juan feels that he lacks class. He both rebels against and envies class. He has, of course, polished charms, but he is suspicious of anyone who readily falls in sway with his practiced ways. He tries to accomplish by achievement what he feels he lacks by birth and breeding. His greatest charm and seductive persuasion reside in his grasping the arbitrariness of existence. In that, Juan realizes that there are no universals that are known or knowable in our experience; truth is, then, persuasion.[14] What a man accepts to be valid or true is simply that which falls in with what he would like to believe is true. He realizes that truth is what men agree to be true. Believing makes it so!

The Noble Savage

Considering Don Juan's inordinate trepidations, from whence comes his strength and his manifest confidence? To understand these matters we must examine the role of the Noble Savage in Don Juan's character.

Despite the depths of discomfort and despair Don Juan has known, there has always existed for him a hidden and inexplicable source of fortitude—a refusal to finally surrender to the forces of hopelessness and inertia. Juan has referred to this fortitude as the voice of the Noble Savage. He tells us of his calling:

> The voice of the Noble Savage speaks to me with a conviction and an urgency from which I cannot escape. He propels me into a quest and a journey for which I feel unprepared, a journey for which I may never be prepared, nonetheless, a journey of which I must and will partake. I have asked myself that if God is dead from whence comes the source of my continued existence? If God is dead how do I exist? I have come to realize that I exist because I *will* to exist. If I should succumb it would be because my will was weaker than the wills that confront and oppose me—be they natural or the

figment of my mind. For in our lives only the will is noble. Will is superior for it is beyond love, sex, pleasure and even happiness. These are weak, sickly passions. Will is beyond good and beyond evil. It is a separate source of itself, it is its own force and stream of life. Will is beyond good and evil as these are terms from an ancient code of morality which has little validity in the modern world. This ancient code has no respect for the emotional and psychological development of the superior. In fact, it does not recognize the individual. It sees only the masses of *mediocrity*. It has eyes only for the degeneration of man. It says "Thou shall *not!*" do this or that, it has no concern for the unique qualities of the individual, nor does it raise man in general. If this morality is injurious to the individual and since God is dead, then, for whom should this code be kept? Unique men must be freed from the restriction of blind supplication to a dead God and a "dead" code which is fitted for only the needs of the mediocre members of society. The Noble Savage must ennoble his Self by purging himself of weak sentimental ties. If my flesh is weak, my mind indecisive, then my will must be built of granite. For will alone exercises the existence of the Self, it alone makes any sense of existence. Only as the Noble Savage lives powerfully, lives dangerously, can he enjoin his full powers, the vital will of his Self. He must place faith in nothing else but his will, for wherever else faith is placed, knowledge is stultified. The will must be exercised and tested to gain the experience of the Self's strength and its capacity for assurgence. Truth is a hard commodity, the heart must be hard, as well. As such, it is better to be a magnificent devil than a sickly angel!

How can Don Juan reconcile the call from his Noble Savage with his trepidation of being uncovered as an ordinary man? Not successfully! Juan's inability to emotionally deal with this dilemma has resulted in a philosophical depression of which Don Juan's critics seem totally unaware.

Philosophical Depression

Philosophical depression stands in contrast to clinical or reactive depression. In this stance the Self is detached from the external world—existing as an observer, romantically "enjoying" its detachment as it offers meaning. It confirms the Self as a "tragic hero," whose meaning resides in its alienation from others, due to their misunderstanding of the intentionality and unique qualities of the Self's being. In philosophical depression the Self experiences itself reaching, stretching, and striving to be all it can, but the Self has no informed direction nor a specific conscious objective for being in the world. Thus, the Self experiences itself at one moment liberated, the next bored and repetitious, and a moment later frightened and enclosed.

Obviously, narcissistic injuries contribute to the choice of philosophical depression. The Self "chooses" philosophical depression, in Juan's case, in opposition to the hysterical demands and worldliness of his mother and the depressive anger of his overly intellectualized, psychologically absent father. The narcissistic injuries, while leaving the Self with its Self-evaluation as less capable, less attractive, less desirable than other Selves, have their concomitant compensatory mechanism. In philosophical depression the Self is sensitized to the illusion and fraud in the lives of other men and the pain that lurks behind these illusions. But because of its experienced helplessness in mitigating and healing others' pain, the Self withdraws from the object world, as Don Juan does in Shaw's interpretation of the legend, and desperately attempts to deny its lost powers, its disintegration to the status and the experience of ordinary beings. When this dissipation can no longer be denied, the Self generally chooses to terminate its existence.

Philosophical depression is intended to fill a void, to avert the terror of uncertainty, to give poetry and meaning to the Self's inability to master and enjoy its being-in-the-world. This depression justifies the Self's refusal to engage in random, desperate, and futile efforts to actively master its world.

The affective qualities of philosophical depression differ from the moods of most people, in that there are wide swings in the evaluation in the Self's appraisal of its worth—giving this stance more of the quality of a cycloid manifestation. It is clearly, in this sense, differentiated from clinical depression. Moreover, despite its cycloid aspect, it rarely reaches the frenzied activities of mania, although in its upswing the psychic energies freed are capable of being drawn into creative endeavors.[15] Bartolomo Venzetti's (1946) written statement to the court in the controversial Sacco-Venzetti trail demonstrates the essence of philosophical depression. Venzetti writes in the final paragraph of his statement:

If it had not been for these things
I might have lived out my life
talking at street corners to scorning men.
I might have died, unmarked, unknown, a failure.
Now we are not a failure.
This is our career and our triumph. Never
in our full life could we hope to do such work
for tolerance, for justice, for man's understanding
of man, as we do by accident.
Our words, our lives, our pains—nothing!
the taking of our lives—lives of a good
        shoemaker and a poor fishpeddler
—all! that last moment belongs to us—
that agony is our triumph.

Philosophical depression transforms the character of Don Juan from simply that of an acting out, ordinary pursuer of the good life into a creative and introspective Self. It also casts Juan from an "ordinary" neurotic into a tragic character. The pathos of Don Juan's saga is his full sense of his destiny— to pursue that which is unattainable, the perfect mother. Don Juan knows her ultimate unattainability, but he cannot avert his quest—he must play out his destiny; he continues to conquer countless women in magical hope of fusing with a more perfect mother.

This is not to say that Don Juan is not without an ironic sense of humor. This aspect of his character was captured so dynamically in the closing scene of the Don Juan movie starring Errol Flynn. Juan tells his sidekick, Leporello, that he is going to change his life style. He will give up his pursuit of women and instead write an epistle about the foolishness of the sensual life. But, of course, he doesn't! He spots a carriage with a ravishingly lovely lady who waves at him, and Juan rides toward her. He explains to his amazed servant that there is a little of Don Juan in every man, and since he is Don Juan, there is naturally more in him. Ah, although he says it with a laugh, the tragic element in Juan's situation is evident. Don Juan refuses to acknowledge what the poet[16] lamented about Narcissus: "Through his own eyes he destroys himself."

Don Juan would have us believe, instead, that he is a joyful dilettante. He is really a victim. He would have us believe that he cares not. Instead, he cares too much! Do we pity Don Juan? He will not let us. Why? He feels undeserving of others' care. His helplessness he experiences as his punishment for a crime he has not committed. And within resides the tragedy of Don Juan. He is no less tragic than Macbeth, but lacks a Shakespeare to plead his case. Juan cannot share himself because he experiences his inner corruption. He must instead get into the bodies and souls of others to avoid opening his pain to others. What Juan fails to appreciate, of course, is his own inner gifts. What he fails to trust is precisely what he states in one form or another to each woman he seduces:

> All I have is my intellect, my body and my soul—that is all I will ever have. Everything else can be bought and sold. All things are meant to be used, not to be imprisoned by. These are the only things worth salvaging and holding onto.

Juan has been told that for all his indulgences he will eventuate old, alone, and unhappy. Juan laughs at this idea. Why wait to be alone and unhappy, he asks, when he can do this while still youthful! This brings us to Don Juan's punishment.

Don Juan's Punishment

As Don Juan becomes alive only in the "turn on" of the other, he dissipates in its absence. He fears that his magic has been rescinded. He feels that his condemnation is now to truly begin. He fears most that his condemnation is to be alone, to be unwanted, and to be laughed at. We hear this in his dialogue of conflict with *el diablo*:

Diablo: Don Juan you will be given the ultimate hell. You will be given the hell of your own selection—the most horrible hell you can imagine! Tell me, Juan, what would be the hell you dread more than all else?

Juan: To live in a place of pure narcissism. All the great narcissists of history and legend—Alexander, Caesar, Narcissus—to be my only companions. And I would have to be at all times a greater narcissist than all the others!

Diablo: No, Juan, there is a far more terrible hell for you! To enable you to choose your own hell you will be given the curse of speaking only truth. What say you, now, Juan!

Juan: My condemnation will be to behold a magnificient woman and not to be able to get it up. That my diablo will be my curse and my damnation!

The Quest for Certainty Versus the Quest for Freedom

Chapter Three

"It isn't the things we like that hurt us, it's our attachment to them (bondage)."
—Hugh Downs

That the narcissistic dilemmas of personality are afflictions of human volition and emotion is rather obvious, as I have tried to demonstrate in previous chapters. Indeed, these are the psychological attributes with which clinicians and psychotherapists generally concern themselves. Notwithstanding, personality theorists, such as Salvadore Maddi (1967), have indicated that personality afflictions, whether neurotic, characterological, or existential, need to be examined in terms of cognitive components, as well as affective and actional attributes. In short, clinical descriptions of the narcissistic condition, for the most part, ignore the attitudinal and cognitive aspects of the narcissistic condition. This is surprising and unfortunate, insofar as there is a rich abundance of empirical data in the areas of developmental, personality, and social psychology on how psychological structures shape the way men attend their world. In this chapter I will discuss these resources, in examining how the Self tries to reduce its neurosis without having to give up its preconceived ideas and emotional myths.

I will begin this essay by asking, "Of what use is a man's freedom?" This may seem to be an inane question. One might well ask in reply: "Isn't it a natural inclination for all men to seek freedom?" Man's quest for his own freedom is a major part of his attempt to meet and master his world. As such, attempts at freedom are integral parts of a man's personality. But we must acknowledge that there are individual differences in personality style. We must contend, therefore, that there are individual differences in man's quest for his own freedom. While most men may prescribe to some ideal state of freedom that they wish to attain, men are not equally capable or desirous of risking chafe and insult in the pursuit of that particular state of freedom.

Before I develop this theme any further, let me say that this chapter is not intended to be a philosophical essay. I contend that the question of freedom is as much a psychological problem as it is philosophical rhetoric. I believe that the principles and conditions underlying psychological freedom are well rooted, although covert, in the developmental, personality, and social psychology literature. In large part, the reason for this neglectful state of affairs is that social scientists, particularly psychologists, have shied away from the problem of freedom in fear of its philosophical contamination; hence, the resulting label of "nonscientific" subject matter.

The position I take, and which I shall discuss in considerable detail in the next chapter, is that freedom is a state of mind. It is our feelings that free or imprison us. Freedom, then, is a psychological term and a psychological problem. The feeling of freedom detracts nothing from determinism as a principle governing human behavior, but is itself causally determined by the realization that one seems to be able, at least in some aspects of one's life, to have some control over one's own behavior.

Nevertheless, while it is true that freedom is a psychological state of affairs and that the feeling one has some control over one's behavior may even be an illusion, it is also true that men act upon their belief in freedom of choice as if it were existentially the case. This is the basis, for example, of holding men responsible for their own actions in legal statutes. As I have said, there are individual differences in each man's quest for his own freedom. If a person believes that he has choice over his own behavior, he generally acts in ways to maximize that choice. If, on the other hand, he believes that he has little choice over his behavior, he generally acts in ways to minimize choice. The underlying reasons for this tendency I believe, can be explained within the dimensions of the quest for certainty and the quest for freedom. These two dimensions may not be mutually exclusive except in their extreme states. A quest for certainty is an extremely exerted effort to maintain a fixed, stable level of organization over one's cognitive system. Similarly, the person who seeks personal freedom is also seeking organization over his cognitive system. He seems more able, however, to withstand disorganization or imbalance, in attempting to gain a new and more complex cognitive organization. More about this presently.

To best distinguish between these two quests, I will employ the concepts of "open" and "closed" mindedness formulated some years ago by Milton Rokeach (1960). It is quite possible that some typology, other than those of Rokeach, would better describe the dynamics involved in the quests for certainty and for freedom. However, I have two reasons for pertaining closely to Rokeach's conceptualizations rather than formulating my own typologies: (1) I believe that the dimensions of behavior that Rokeach describes correspond reasonably closely to my own interests; and (2) a great deal of research has been conducted along the lines of Rokeach's typologies, while the findings of many other studies can be conveniently converted into Rokeach's terms. Use of the concepts of open and closed mindedness, then, will afford us access to a rich store of empirical data upon which to test my contentions.

To begin with, if we are to legitimately contend that individuals differ in their quest for freedom and that this quest flows in a consistent way from basic personality styles—which Rokeach has called "open" and "closed" mindedness—I am pressed at some point to indicate the function served by adopting these particular personality styles. The simplest explanation for the employment of a personality style is that it is a *strategy* the individual employs in organizing his world and committing himself to that organization. This is to say, the only way we can "know" the world is through our sense receptors. Since there is no direct correlation between the external world and the information we receive from our senses, we live by necessity in a world of uncertainty. In order to move successfully through our world, we cannot hope to depend on absolute truth about how the external world is constituted, but are forced to make inferences about the accuracy of the information we receive from our senses. In organizing their world, it is also characteristic of all individuals to order goals that designate what they prefer and what they would like to avoid.

What are personality styles, then? They are commitments to withstand a certain degree of anxiety and uncertainty in the quest of the goals that inform our existence (Goldberg, 1973). Basically, I believe that each individual can be described as holding relatively consistently flexible or inflexible strategies, along what Rokeach has described as an open–closed minded continuum.

In clinical terms, the closed-minded strategies are defensive. They are largely inflexible and are generally isolated from one another; that is, closed-minded people often hold beliefs that are logically inconsistent with one another. Closed-minded people seem to be incapable or unwilling to withstand high degrees of anxiety or cognitive disorganization, which are inherent in situations that are cognitively complex, ambiguous, or involve considerable uncertainty of outcome. Because anxiety is easily aroused in such situations, closed-minded people seek situations where quick, easy, and absolutely "correct" behavior can be readily anticipated. The strategy they seem to characteristically employ when called upon to interpret situations is to use familiar, reliable, and stereotypical responses, or for that matter, any response that does not involve a great deal of uncertainty of outcome. Close-minded people are also not easily able to shift, readjust, or change their customary way of responding in novel situations, because the use of novel and untried responses involves considerable uncertainty. Thus, in avoiding new and cognitively complex situations in order to maximize certainty of outcome, close-minded behavior does not always seem realistic from the outside, and may seem to be more of a reaction to the situation than an involvement with and participation in the situation.

It would also seem possible to talk about closed-minded persons as people who believe that they have little or no freedom of choice over their behavior. This belief serves as a rationalization for their attempts to minimize choice over their own behavior. The more freedom of choice one ascribes to one's own behavior, the more uncertainty one is faced with in choosing any of the alternatives brought into awareness. However, in traveling under the assumption that one has little or no choice over behavior, one risks little or nothing by not actively choosing from among a larger, and by definition, more anxiety-producing repertoire. Consequently, if one chooses a customary response in any given situation, one can expect with some certainty that what will happen will be what has happened in the past when the same response was employed. Thus, closed-minded individuals, in experiencing choice over their own anxiety-producing behavior, attempt to minimize their freedom of choice.

The motives that lead to the employment of open and closed-minded strategies are, of course, learned. They develop out of the repeated affective experiences connected with situations and kinds of behavior involving "standards of expected behavior" imposed upon the child by society, or more particularly, by his parents as representatives of society. These strategies are employed to respond to standards of expected behavior which, if met successfully, produce positive affect and, if noncompleted, will evoke negative affect for the child.

First, we must realize that the parents hold considerable power in regard to the child's behavior. At the beginning of a child's life, nearly all the controls of his change-worthy actions come from his parents (Sears, Maccoby, and Levin, 1957). The parents possess and control the material and emotional supplies craved by the child. Through manipulation of these supplies, the parents can potentially force any behavior on the child, within the limitations of the child's biological and intellectual capacity. The parents' choice of techniques is almost unlimited, and we can reasonably expect to find a relation between the parents' own personalities and their manner of interacting with their child.

Control of the child may be enacted most directly by the use of influence-techniques that rely on external pressure, rather than on the child's own controls. The most clear-cut controlling techniques are those that convey to the child that he must, without question, change his entire ongoing pattern of behavior immediately, giving no explanation for the demand and making no attempt to compensate the child for the resulting deprivation.

Several aspects of the authoritarian syndrome, upon which Rokeach's work is derived, stand out as having a bearing on the parents' power assertion toward their child. First, we would expect the authoritarian's value on power and status, rather than understanding and consideration of the child's needs, to be expressed directly in the frequent use of power-assertive techniques in trying to change the child's behavior. The authoritarian's orientation toward power and status is also reflected, at a somewhat deeper level, in the tendency to identify with high-power roles and not with low-power roles. In disciplining the child, we should expect the authoritarian parent to show little empathy and consideration for the child's feelings. Instead of qualifying his demands, explaining them, or compensating the child for cessation of his ongoing behavior, the authoritarian parent focuses on the child's compliance. Moreover, the authoritarian's characteristic defensiveness against anxiety and doubt elicits in the authoritarian parent a relatively high degree of self-confidence in the correctness of his disciplinary approach, further reducing the likelihood of his seeking to understand the child's position, to explain demands, or to provide compensatory gratification in regard to those things the child desires. In short, then, the authoritarian parent's power and status orientation, his tendency to identify with a high-power role, and his defensiveness against doubt contribute to the use of unqualified power-assertive techniques when the child does not live up to the standards of behavior expected by the parent.

The evaluation of a child's behavior also will be influenced by what the parent feels the child's behavior reflects about his or her adequacy as a parent. The authoritarian's self-image as an adequate parent is apt to be bound up, to a considerable degree, with his or her ability to command respect and unquestioned obedience from the child. The child's noncompliance may then pose a personal threat to the authoritarian parent. The authoritarian's demands on the young child force the child to make a binary choice between only two behaviors—compliance or noncompliance. The choice is rather straightforward for the child of an authoritarian parent, in that there is little risk of uncertainty in regard to the outcomes of these choices. The child, early in his existence, becomes aware of the clearly differentiated parental reaction to each of the child's choices. It is unlikely that the authoritarian parent will perceive the healthy or necessary aspect of non-compliance for the child's developing ego and sense of autonomy, much less experience any pride in occasional acts of defiance.

We are now touching upon one of the more salient factors in differentiating open and closed-minded persons. Nonauthoritarian parents are more likely to permit their child to rebel. While they may not realize that occasional acts of rebellion are healthy indications of developing maturity by the child, at least they are less likely to perceive rebellion as a threat to their own conception of themselves as adequate parents. The child's experience of rebellion greatly modifies his authority relationship with parents and other adults. This occasion for partial noncompliance with authority's demands becomes an opportunity for the child to experience a greater variety of alternatives to behavior, creating greater complexity in the parent-child relationship. It confronts each authoritative expectation with three alternatives: (1) a response to conform to the demand; (2) a response to acquiesce to a punishment for noncompliance; and (3) to not acquiesce to either component of the "either-or" parental demand. Thus, rebellion makes the environment of authority more complex by imposing an additional option to the simple "either-or" confrontation of parental demands. The child that is too frightened to rebel is not afforded increased freedom in a situation and is forced to either acquiesce or be punished.

The discussion heretofore has described how the authoritarian parent views his relationship with his child and the techniques he employs to ensure desired reactions from the child. But how are these techniques perceived and reacted to by the child? It might be helpful to conceptualize the authoritarian parent-child realtionship as a system of communication by which the child learns and tries out strategies in order to interpret and master his world.

It is assumed that every communication received from an external authority source contains two kinds of information. It contains information of a substantive nature, and it contains information about the authority source itself. Substantive information is typically obtained from the sheer content of the message. The child with an authoritarian parent soon learns to disregard nuances, mitigating circumstances, or special considerations in interpersonal situations—in other words, the objective reality of the situations—because he has learned that the parent has less concern for the child's evaluation of the situation than he does in unquestioned obedience from the child. Since the authoritarian parent rarely offers an accompanying explanation for a demand, the child is rarely aware of the appropriateness of parental wishes in relation to the situation, or how many other choices, aside from the one demanded by the parent, are possible to him, if he were to disregard his parents' demands. The child "discovers" that the correctness or incorrectness of expected behavior rests entirely upon the parents' whims.

To maximize the certainty of acting correctly in interpersonal situations, the child is forced to sensitize himself in discovering precisely what the parents' wishes are in any particular situation.

In sum, then, in order to maximize the certainty of being "correct," the child is forced to sensitize himself to high-power (authoritarian) sources, rather than low-power sources. The great philosophical discovery of his life is his realization that the world consists of "hammers" and "nails." There are two kinds of people in the world—those who "hammer" and those who get "hammered." In order to maximize the certainty of being re-warded, instead of being "hammered," he is forced to attend to those pow-erful figures who, he has learned from early childhood, inevitably get their way.

As I have already discussed, the authoritarian parent presents his child at an early age with only two alternatives to behavior. As the child grows older, however, situations become more complex for the child. The parent cannot always be with the child, interpreting the choices for him. The inexperienced child is thus often faced with a multiplicity of choices, which confuses him and evokes considerable anxiety for him. The child in such sit-uations may well wish he could return to a more infantile period, in which choices were far clearer. In search for a simple and reliable frame of refer-ence, the child of an authoritarian parent generally closes himself off to all aspects of a communication system other than the identification of the source. If the parent had been a dependable frame of reference in the past, the child expects with some certainty that other high-power sources may be dependable frames of reference in the present. The more the individual sen-sitizes his orientation toward the source, and not to its content, the less will the two kinds of information be clearly distinguished from each other, and the less each will be evaluated and responded to in terms of their respective merits. This is what is meant by "closed mindedness." A person has the ca-pacity to choose whether or not to be influenced by information presented by a source to the extent that he can clearly distinguish the content of the communication from the power of the source. The greater one's orientation with authority, the more difficult this cognitive task will be, by virtue of the authority's effective capacity to simplify choice. What the external au-thority says is true about the world becomes cognitively indistinguishable from what the external authority wants us to believe is true, and wants us to do about it.

In short, the contention I have been arguing is that the way beliefs are structured, restructured, and maintained by the individual is closely related to the quality of the individual's cognitive functioning. There is consid-erable empirical support for this contention. Two studies will be men-tioned. Kutner (1958) found that children who demonstrated a high degree of group prejudice correspondingly exhibited a number of cognitive difficulties in dealing with objective tasks. Their performance was characterized by a tendency toward rigidity, overgeneralization, categorizing, dichotomizing, concretization, simplification, dogmatism, and intolerance for ambiguity. The less prejudiced children exhibited a tendency toward flexibility, realistic generalization, individualization, abstraction, retention of complexity, totality, a lack of dogmatism, and a tolerance for ambiguity. Klein (1963), in studying the problem-solving ability of college students, found a consistent negative correlation between concept formulation and authoritarianism and between deductive reasoning and authoritarianism.

What I have discussed so far is still an overview of manifest cognitive functioning. To better understand how open and closed-minded persons differ in their strategies in mastering their world, one must investigate the cognitive process itself.

One of the universally accepted statements derived from psychological investigation posits that the psychological tendency is that of structuring of experience. There is an inherent tendency in human experience to structure present objects and events (perception) and, similarly, in the experience of objects and events not immediately present (remembering, imagining, and so forth), we tend to see definite forms and patterns. In time our memory of them may be modified or transformed, yet still further structured (Goldberg, 1977a). Heider (1957) has described this psychological tendency toward structuring as cognitive balance. A state of psychological harmony exists if entities which are perceived as belonging together are all positive or if they are all negative. If closely related entities are of different signs, then a state of tension or disharmony exists. This state of disharmony can be resolved in several ways, as was shown in an experiment by Jordan (1953). He presented a vast array of combinations of balanced and imbalanced situations to subjects and asked them to rate them for imagined experience of pleasure. He found that when a person finds himself in an unbalanced situation, forces act upon him to achieve balance, and that the rating of pleasantness is a function of balance plus the existence of a gratifying social relationship between two people in a situation; whereas unpleasantness is a function of imbalance.

There is much more to cognitive functioning, of course, than a simple process of structuring and balance. There is the intriguing matter of cognitive complexity. Cognitive complexity refers to psychological structuring or reorganizaton of perception, memory, or imagination due to the processing of greater (new) stimulus input. This might occur, for example, when a person discovers a new way of solving a difficult problem by being able to respond to a greater number of dimensions in the situation than he could originally, one of which may be the essential component required to solve the problem. According to Bieri (1961), a system of constructs that differentiates selectively among persons is considered to be cognitively complex.

A system of constructs that discriminates poorly among persons, on the other hand, is considered to be cognitively simple in structure. Closed-minded people, in employing stereotypical and oversimplified strategies in responding to the external world, reflect structural simplification in their cognitive systems. An accurate perception of other people, for example, is a function of one's predictive accuracy about others' behavior. This predictive behavior is assumed by Bieri to be dependent upon interpersonal discriminations or constructs the perceiver invokes in making his predictions. The complexity of an individual's cognitive system is relative to the degree of differentiation among his perceptions of others. The individual who makes poor discriminations is more likely to assume that others are the same as he is and, on the basis of this projection, fuse his own intentions as an inaccurate prediction of others. The person who makes finer discriminations is less likely to engage in projection in his perceptions of other individuals. In making greater differentiation of others, he is more likely to perceive how they differ from himself, and, thus avoiding projection, he can more objectively predict their behavior. From this description we may be better able to understand why open-minded people are less prejudiced, in general, than are closed-minded people. By less prejudiced, I mean being less predisposed to prejudicing others in a stereotypical, general way, apart from specific characteristics of the person, and apart from specific instances of behavior. Open-minded people, in being able to perceive more differences between people, are able to use more alternatives in classifying people and differentiating their behavior. Open-minded people, in being more cognitively complex, are able to react to more appropriate alternatives in each situation, rather than employing old, stereotypical responses that are less appropriate for the new situation.

This increased cognitive complexity, however, further complicates the situation. As we might suspect from Jordan's study, since new stimulus input or cognitive complexity may be divergent with existing patterns of psychological structuring, it seems reasonable that the individual may experience discomfort and anxiety in trying to maintain a disharmonious cognitive system. Studies such as Aronson and Carlsmith's (1963), for example, have shown that if a person expects to perform poorly in a particular endeavor, effecting a good performance will be inconsistent with his expectation, and he will attempt to reduce cognitive dissonance by denying the performance. This is, indeed, what I suspect happens with closed-minded persons. In situations in which they are aware of a large number of dimensions to the situation, they are correspondingly faced with a variegation of choices. Finding choice anxiety-producing—since greater risk is encountered by choosing from among a variety of new alternatives rather than from a few fixed, reliable choices—the closed-minded person attempts to minimize risk and maximize certainty by cognitively denying the new alternatives and responding only to the habitual choices. Suppression, then, is a common means of achieving cognitive harmony for the closed-minded person. Consequently, in situations where choice and its accompaniment, anxiety, are present, the Self suppresses information, mitigating against changes in belief systems that are cognitively disruptive.

How applicable is the delineation of cognitive functioning discussed above? This is to say, if we accept Heider, Jordan, and Aronson and Carlsmith's findings, how can we account for the ostensible observation that some individuals at times disrupt cognitive balance in the interest of seeking greater stimulus input, such as the creative individuals investigated by Barron (1968)? A step in the direction of answering this question may have been elicited in a study conducted by the Psychiatric Department of the Cincinnati General Hospital several years ago. Investigators found that the creative child is likely to come from a home and a family which they characterized as loosely organized, not overly intimate nor particularly well adjusted. Each parent perceives the marriage and family life in somewhat different terms. It is a family in which there is open and not always calm expression of strong/feelings, without, however, that expression being used to bind the child to the values of either parent. Nor does either parent use the child against the other parent to prove himself a better parent or person. In this environment a child is able to develop an adaptive, reconstructive strategy learned early in childhood, in which he can regress to a more primitive stage of development without fear of disapproval from his parents. On the other hand, regression and withdrawal were not primary means of dealing with an anxiety-producing environment by the creative individuals studied. Rather, this creative individual, who we recognize as an open-minded person by his flexibility and behavioral adaptiveness, had been conditioned to tolerate a high degree of ambiguity (for example, inconsistency in parental values), without this ambiguity having a disruptive effect on his cognitive processing of new information. The open-minded person—faced with the need to discriminate, not only among alternate behaviors but also among varying expectations about similar or identical behavior, and feeling no compunction to act in any particular way—experiences choice, if not as a comfortable state of affairs, then at least one with a minimum of duress. The open-minded person, relatively free of disruptive anxiety in situations of high ambiguity, is capable of employing the cognitive complexity inherent in a situation to create greater novelty and innovative restructuring of his cognitive organization—without experiencing the need to defend himself against anxiety. Bieri and Blacker's (1956) study confirms what common sense purports: that the more differentiated a cognitive system is relative to the person's perception of external events—that is, the more alternative perceptions of an event available—the more alternative behaviors will be available to that situation. Thus, as the open-minded person perceives greater differentiation among situations, he is likely to become more critical in his choice of particular responses. As he becomes more critical, he is also more apt to avert arbitrary and conventional choices and sensitize himself to discovering inherent standards that govern nature, in so doing gain a greater mastery of his world.

In that this volume is concerned with the interface of Self and society, it would be useful to relate what I have already discussed with the concepts of conformity and social deviation. This is to say, how is the conceptualization of open and closed-mindedness related to the study of individual differences in the acceptance of group norms?

It seems rather evident that closed-minded people are drawn toward groups in which social norms are clearly discernible and are not overly flexible. Flexibility incurs ambiguity. Ambiguity equals choice. Choice involves risk. Risk generates a high amount of anxiety. As we have already demonstrated, closed-minded people avoid anxious situations. Closed-minded people also are attracted by authoritarian leaders who exert considerable pressure to conform. These are social settings in which choice is minimized and certainty maximized, by employing fixed, stable, and reliable frames of reference learned in childhood.

The question remains: have closed-minded people really accepted group norms in the way I have defined "acceptance," that is, as an internalization of norms? Rather than the individual feeling himself interned, he feels that he, himself, has appropriated the value? In addition, is there any implication that the individual accepts these values because they are consistent with his beliefs of what one *should* do in any specific situation, rather than conforming to the group norm because he will either be rewarded or negatively sanctioned if he doesn't act in such a way as the group wishes him?

According to the consensus of studies in the literature, the closed-minded people conform to group norms because resistance to authority would force the individual to seek new alternatives to behavior, which are too risky for him to handle. It has been shown by Smith (1961), for example, that resistance to group pressure is dependent upon the person's capacity to assimilate discrepancies in information input without being threatened. We already know that closed-minded people are incapable of this ability. Thus, in order for the closed-minded person to master his world, he must depend upon information that is consistent with his existing cognitive system. Closed-minded people, therefore, only conform in order to survive (reduce anxiety to tolerable levels); but the evidence seems to show that they don't like the mode they have adopted and so may rebel in subtle but significant ways.

Hoffman (1957) has indicated that when a person yields to group opinion in expressing a judgment, he may be expressing a generalized need to be in agreement with the group rather than responding exclusively to some aspect of the situation. Hoffman has also demonstrated, according to his report, that a high conformity–need subject, as compared to a low conformity–need subject, has less anxiety when he conforms to a norm that diverges from his own view, than when he maintains his initial response in the face of such a norm; has less anxiety when the norm agrees with him all along, than when he maintains his initial response in the face of a divergent norm; and has more anxiety when he conforms to a divergent norm, than when the norm agrees all along. Hoffman feels that his data support the notion of conformity as a defense against anxiety. That is, Hoffman feels that under certain circumstances, conforming behavior can avoid rather than just reduce anxiety and that it can actually function as a form of resistance to genuine group influence. Breger (1963) reports that he found conformity to be part of an ego-defensive process centered around repression of hostility. Crowne and Liverant (1963) also seem to support this contention. In general, they found that conformers were lacking social confidence, had low expectations of success in situations of social evaluation, and where, for the main, found to employ failure-avoidant, self-protective behavior, all apt descriptions of closed-minded persons.

To explain why closed-minded people are likely to conform to but not accept group norms, one must remember that in Rokeach's system, cognitive and emotional processes are closely allied. Use of Frenkel-Brunswik's (1974) "personality-centered approach to perception" can help serve us better to see this relationship. Her main thesis, derived from psychoanalysis, is that there exists an interrelationship between cognitive spheres of behavior, on the one hand, and the emotion and social spheres, on the other. She starts with the psychoanalytic concept of emotional ambivalence and the role it plays in the development of the child. She develops the notion that as a result of early parent-child relations, involving varying degrees of permissiveness or punitiveness, there emerge individual differences in the ability to tolerate emotional ambivalence toward parents which, in turn, "spill over" into the social and cognitive spheres as well. Thus, a child who, through punishment, is not permitted to express his normal ambivalent feelings—as we saw happen to the child of an authoritarian parent—develops a generalized need to structure his world rigidly, a pervasive tendency to premature closure, and a general intolerance of cognitive ambiguity. Attempts, for example, to master feelings of aggression toward parental figures, who are experienced as too threatening and powerful to express one's real feelings toward openly, then, are among the important determinants of the tendency to rigidly avoid ambiguity of any sort. The child, under these conditions, may be saying silently to himself, in regard to his parents: "You can make me act any way you like, so I won't be hurt by you, but you can't make me like it, believe that it is right, or even stop me from hating you."

This may also partially explain why the closed-minded person disregards low-power sources. Having been forced to comply to power-assertive techniques by high-power sources, his resentment needs some outlet. He may find that displacing some of his resulting resentment by resisting the influence-attempts by other less powerful persons is satisfying.

In a sense, then, conformity to authority is a way of getting people one hates and fears "off your back." To the closed-minded, anxiety-prone person, it may be the price he is willing to pay for the small comfort of doing what others ask of him, but *not really believing in it*.

Consequently, I believe that people do not internalize norms, although they may ostentatiously conform to them, unless they experience choice in the matter. What this means, then, is that some individuals give up some of the certainty of success in their behavior, in so doing experiencing anxiety, in order to gain more personal freedom over their behavior. Other people give up most of their own choice over their behavior in order to maximize certainty of acting successfully and to reduce anxiety. Nevertheless, personal freedom seems to be a natural desire of all men, and those who have surrendered it, for whatever consideration, feel frustration and resentment at its loss. This frustration seems to be kindled by the feeling that part of one's potential as a fully experiencing, purposive human being is being denied.

I ask you, then, what is your commitment to be—toward freedom, or toward certainty!

Chapter Four

The Function Of

Human Will

"If I'm not for myself, who will for me?
If I'm for myself alone, what am I?
If not now, when?"

—Rabbi Hillel

Jan Linthorst (1975), a theologian and a psychotherapist, argues that a great many of modern man's psychological dilemmas are derived from his lack of appreciation of will in human endeavor. According to Linthorst, freedom is commonly regarded as

> the same as autonomy and consequently man, seeking meaning, happiness and security in his life, asserts himself in willful action to achieve this .... This assertive, action-oriented man [for example] when confronted with a crisis, seeks to solve his problem by approaching the situation in much the same way and since this approach has gotten him into the problem in the first place, he only compounds his problem, beating against a wall even harder.

Have we, as social scientists, prematurely abandoned the concept of conscious will and have as a result abetted in incapacitating modern man from regulating his own existence? If so, what does the abandonment of human will mean in terms of present prescriptions of human behavior, and what does it reveal about contemporary concepts of human nature (Goldberg, 1977[b])?

There are four major intentions in the following chapter: First, to stress the importance of reviving the study of human will in the social sciences; second, to infuse academic psychology and clinical psychology with existential and phenomenological epistemology; third, to emphasize the need to recognize intentionality as integral in the development of Self (personality); and, fourth, to delineate the developmental phases of will, so that the clinician may be aware of his client's ontological struggle in seeking meaning in his existence.

Have American psychology and psychiatry prematurely abandoned the concept of will in explaining human behavior?

During the first two centuries of thought in our country, volition played a central role in interpreting human behavior. No other single psychological concept drew as much interest or produced as many volumes and scholarly theses. The faculty of will drew the attention not only of psychologists, but also of philosophers, theologians, educators, and practitioners of jurisprudence, because it stood at the crossroads of several disciplines and was regarded as the springboard of human action (Roback, 1964).

Gradually, in an effort to establish an empirical science, American psychology began to reject the language, concepts, and philosophical foundations of European psychology. With increasing emphasis being given to unconscious motivation, along with the role of environmental factors, free will was regarded as unnecessary to explain human behavior. The abandonment of volition marked a new epoch in American psychology:

> It is only in the last century that human behavior has been viewed as a complex integration of basic biological needs and essential cultural adaptations. Previously man was understood as having animal needs and a spiritual nature endowed by God which gave him the capacity to choose between right and wrong and good and bad. [Salzman, 1974]

In attributing greater complexity to human behavior, psychology at the same time has deprived the individual of purpose. A discussion of such concepts as will, volition, purpose, and psychological freedom was once regarded as indispensable to an intelligent inquiry into human affairs, but since the 1930s these concepts have virtually disappeared from the subject matter and textbooks of psychology (Gilbert, 1970).

Difficulties Encountered when the Concept of Will is Abandoned

Casting aside the concept of human will presents several serious difficulties in both the description and the prescription of human behavior. My first objection to discarding will is epistemological.

Personality theory is deficient without a unifying concept that takes human purpose and intent into account. The jettison of human will has resulted in some current personality theories that posit extreme distortions of volitional behavior. At one extreme, some theorists attempt to explain human behavior by totally rejecting the presence of human purpose and choice. This view is exemplified in the early behaviorism of Watson (1914), in the sophisticated operant-learning theories of Skinner (1971), and in complex and dynamic psychoanalytic theory as interpreted by such practitioners as Knight (1946) and Menninger (1958).

However, psychologists are prone to discard concepts under one name and retrieve them later under another (Royce, 1970). Some theorists have made covert attempts to account for purposive human action by describing dynamics that resemble volitional behavior. Such terms as "self-actualization," "self-consistency," "trend toward autonomy," "ego-syntonic," and "striving for superiority," which are proposed as innate attributes, help to organize the behavior of some people but appear to be unaccountably deficient for others. On the other hand, theorists who have openly employed the term "will" in their formulations of psychological functioning have not gained respectability in academic circles or acceptance among the clinicians for whom Rank (1945), Low (1952), and Assagioli (1974) originally formulated their theories.

Without taking human will into account, it is difficult to regard the unfolding of personality as a Self in search of meaning for its existence. Furthermore, the denial of purpose in psychological theory is a contradiction of ordinary observation. Willing and choice are matters of everyday experience. Theories of personality that deny human will are therefore both misleading and insufficient. In his critique on the role of determinism in the social sciences, Mullahy (1949) stated:

> A method or a theory which ignores or explains away the part of its subject-matter which it cannot deal with is or can be in the long run worse than useless. It may raise false hopes and it may mislead if it promises what it cannot fulfill.

A second objection to the repudiation of will is the *moral* one.

Science does not exist in an ethical vacuum. If the nature of its inquiry is selected without regard to a hierarchy of values, it becomes at best naive and aimless, at worst susceptible to destructive exploitation. If the human race is to survive, there must be priorities in science's search for means to enhance significant human values. Accounts of human behavior that disregard the experience of choice and freedom, because these experiences appear not to adhere to science's basic assumptions, may easily fall prey to subjugating forces in our society. We all know of "therapeutic" enterprises that have employed laboratory-verified behavior therapy to inflict the most inhumane regimens of psychological control. I agree with Rollo May (1974) that we must rediscover the function and importance of human will "to deepen human experience, to place these phenomena on a level which would reflect more adequately a dignity and respect for human life."

My third objection is on *pragmatic* grounds.

Scientific discussion about the role of free will in human behavior has self-fulfilling societal implications. Formerly, concepts of theology and natural science were regarded as relevant for explaining human nature. At present, social-science explanations have higher credibility among the general populace. The attitudes of social scientists about the function of volition serve as guidelines for others. Both individuals and social institutions use these attributes to define the range of possibility within which the individual has the freedom to be responsible for his own actions. Wheelis's classic statement of the status of human will and its implications for other human attributes, such as courage and determination, address this concern:

> The unconscious is heir to the prestige of will. As one's fate formerly was determined by will, now it is determined by the repressed in mental life. Knowledgeable moderns put their backs to the couch, and in so doing may fail occasionally to put their shoulders to the wheel. As will has been devalued, so has courage; for courage can exist only in the service of will, and can hardly be valued higher than that which it serves. In our understanding of human nature we have gained determinism, lost determination. [1956]

Can We Investigate the Concept of Will?

To legitimize the concept of will as a proper subject for psychologic investigation, we need to ask if the question of will is accessible to empirical study. Most theorists have contended that human will is inaccessible to empirical investigation and therefore is not a proper study for psychological inquiry (Lapsley, 1967). I suggest that this contention is still open to question.

Proponents of determinism claim that psychology (or any other science) can be a science only to the extent that it accepts a deterministic proposition as its underlying assumption. In other words, if psychology chooses "prediction" as one of the objectives of the game it wishes to play, it must then posit that the relationships between events are bound together in a causal sequence. Proponents of free will have claimed that when this line of reasoning is accepted, there is no longer room for free human activity. Indeed, the psychoanalyst Robert Knight (1946) argued for a strict deterministic view of behavior, contending that the sense of freedom experienced after selecting a course of action and carrying it to fulfillment is an illusion; it has "nothing whatever to do with free will as a principle governing human behavior but is a subjective experience which is itself causally determined."

Heinz Kohut has taken issue with the contention that freedom is an epiphenomenon. His very clear use of psychoanalytic method suggests a means for reopening the issue of free will to empirical investigation:

> Some of the confusion may perhaps be reduced if we again approach the problem by clearly defining the observational method by which we obtain the raw material for our theoretical abstractions. For a science [psychoanalysis] that obtains its observational material through introspection and empathy, the question may be formulated as follows: we can observe in ourselves the ability to choose and to decide—can further introspection [resistance analysis] resolve this ability into underlying components? The opposite psychological configurations, namely the experience of being compelled and the experience of [for example, obsessional] indecision and doubt, can usually be broken down by means of introspection. As we succeed, however, to reduce these phenomena psychoanalytically by establishing their motives, we move simultaneously toward the re-establishment of free choice and decision. Can we do the same with the introspectively observed capability of choice? Can we, by introspection, resolve the experience of making a choice into the components of compulsion and narcissism? The answer to this question is no, despite the emphasis that psychoanalysis puts on unconscious motivation and rationalization; for all that the persistent recovery of unconscious motivations and of rationalizations leads to is, under favorable circumstances, a wider and more vivid experience of freedom. [Kohut, 1959]

Kohut's methodological answer is supported by Mazer's pragmatic approach. Mazer (1960) offers the observation that the analyst's "inhibiting belief in determinism ends at the door of the consulting room." When interacting with family and friends, the analyst "assumes that they are able to transcend at least some of the psychological determinants of their behavior or that the determinants are not powerful." Undoubtedly this is also true of behaviorists.

My position is that freedom of will is a state of being that is made possible by the belief in psychological freedom. The freedom that we experience is derived from the fact that exercising our belief in psychological freedom enables us to act, rather than remain passive. "Freedom" is thus a psychological term and a psychological issue. The belief in freedom does not detract anything from determinism as a principle governing human behavior, but is itself causally determined by the realization that one seems to be able, at least in some aspects of life, to have some control over one's behavior. Psychological freedom, then, implies the principle of causality—that is, behavioral antecedents of some measure of control over one's own behavior.

In reality, the most simple human actions could not be performed in a indeterministic universe. To say that I could have acted differently actually amounts to saying that I would have behaved differently had my prior experiences and the conditions bearing upon me, in conjunction with how I deliberated, been different. Since I am not a chemical salad that changes its structure perpetually or is unaffected by experience, I act with some consistency. Nevertheless, each situation I enter is somewhat different from any other I have experienced, affording new possibilities *if* I seek them out. The effects of these possibilities cannot be ascertained in advance, because the possibilities cannot come into being for me until I turn toward them. The idea of "turning toward possibility" is integral to the function of human will.

I view the manifestation of will as the Self's attempt to express and function as a person it seeks to be in terms of its intentions and actions in the world. (The idea of "intentions and actions in the world" refers to behaviors enacted by the Self with the prospect that other Selves may become aware of them.) However, as Fromm (1963) long ago observed, each person may seek some ideal state of freedom, but people are not equally capable or desirous of enduring anxiety and discomfort in pursuit of psychological freedom. Thus, people act on their belief or disbelief in freedom of choice as if their particular belief were unquestionably valid. If a person believes that he has some choice over his own behavior, he generally acts in ways to maximize that choice. If, on the other hand, he believes that he has little or no choice, he generally acts in ways to minimize it.

In seeking to exercise will, each Self finds itself from moment to moment on a continuum. This extends from seeking freedom, in order to exercise choice, to maximizing certainty by denying the experience of freedom. These quests are not mutually exclusive except in extreme or pathologic states (Goldberg, 1973). To reiterate, then, a need for certainty is an inordinate effort to maintain a fixed, stable organization of the Self's experience in the world. A person who seeks freedom is also seeking organization, but the Self is able during this quest to withstand varying degrees of disorganization and imbalance in attempting to gain a more meaningful existence.

If I were an academic psychologist, I might at this juncture in the chapter endeavor to elaborate and substantiate my descriptions of quests toward freedom and certainty with empirical data. As a clinician, however, I am more concerned about bringing current knowledge of the impairment of the expression of freedom into a systematic frame of reference that enables clients to more fully fulfill their human potential. This raises the pragmatic concern that if the notion of human will is more than merely an epiphenomenon, then the individual in contemporary society requires some conceptual tools to meaningfully understand and take hold of his volitional faculties. Our increasing awareness of the influences on the development and nuturing of Self suggests that there are several stages in the development of human will. In short, findings from psychodynamic studies of personality indicate that, to the extent that unconscious motivation exists, then simple willfulness, or training of the will—as with former conceptions of will—is not sufficient to modify the inability of the Self to will; the Self is not aware of what it is unaware of and avoiding. The Self that cannot get into itself, in order to come to know itself, has no sense of its intentionality, 2nd consequently, no means of directing its being-in-the-world.

Both the conditions that facilitate and those that inhibit the freedom of will have pragmatic consequences for the practitioner. As a therapist, I have become increasingly aware of various influences and task requirements in the development of my patients' ability and willingness to experience freedom of will. I would like to offer a conceptual scheme consisting of four separate but interrelated phases in the development of will, as this relates to the Self's potential for experience and action.

1. *The willingness to be aware of possibility.* It is inaccurate to speak of the presence of will before the Self is aware of need. Human will has typically been regarded as a negating force to repress instinctual demands. While will may frequently function in this capacity, its deeper meaning has to do with the Self's attempt to define its place in the world. The will, as such, derives all its power and direction from the Self's concerns and purposes (Lapsley, 1967). The various projections that the Self casts of itself on the world consist of attitudes and intents of how the Self seeks to be known; taken together, these projections are called the "intentionality" of Self. To the extent that its intentionality remains unconscious, the Self cannot get into itself and is thus forced to avoid itself. This avoidance is a denial of both the desire and possibility of the freedom to express itself in the world. As such, the Self's efforts at willing prove futile.

In this first phase, the Self's developmental task is to close itself off from the world to concentrate on its own internal striving, especially in relation to its bodily being. Early developmental experience—in which considerable emphasis was placed on external power and status, rather than on understanding and consideration of the Self's feelings and inner needs—contributes to impaired ability to close off from the external world. The Self learns that it is not useful—indeed it is painful—to look inside and experience want or heightened feelings. It is less painful and more dependable, and leads to greater certainty of external reward for the Self, to identify with high-power and status objects.

The developmental task of this first phase is resolved by focusing on the bodily sensations of the Self in its existence in the world. The phrases that refer to will as having a physical presence, such as "taking a viewpoint" and "changing an orientation," reveal will as the embodied expression of Self (May, 1974). The Self, divorced from its own intentionality, can, by responding to its somatic communication, gain experiential awareness of the postures it assumes. With increasing bodily awareness, the intent of these postures becomes evident.

2. *The willingness to seek possibility.* Awareness of its inner strivings is not sufficient to enable the Self to function purposely. The developmental task in the second phase is for the Self to become open to external possibility. In opening itself, the Self must make a commitment to withstand varying degrees of discomfort and risk in questioning the validity of certain of its assumptions about the external world.

The world in which we live—when stripped of the myriad of theory, explanation, and preconceived notions—is a big, booming, buzzing confusion. There is no direct correlation between the objective dimensions of the world and what registers on our sense receptors. In order to engage and come to terms with the complexity of our world—or even to survive within the confusion that engulfs our thoughts and feelings—we must make some semblance of meaning from our sensory and kinesthetic experiences. Although we have no assurance that our interpretation of experience is correct, we are constantly compelled to make inferences about what is going on in the world around us. Inferences that concern our physical and psychological safety, shaping the very manner in which we perceive the universe, are called *core attitudes*. These attitudes comprise our sense of Self and of others, shaping the very manner in which we perceive the universe.

We generally respond to the universe in a dual manner. We behave in a way that is intended to achieve a preferred state of affairs; at the same time we act in such a way as to confirm our core attitudes about what we have predicted would happen as a result of our actions. Often we achieve confirmation of our inferences at the expense of our personal freedom. When we avoid situations that are complex or ambiguous or require weighing of possibilities, our expectations about ourselves are confirmed. We acquire a sense of certainty, because the confirmation allows us to believe, however mistakenly, that we are being taken care of in the precarious world we inhabit. The quests for freedom and for certainty, then, are commitments to withstand varying degrees of discomfort and risk in the individual's attempt to organize his world and commit himself to the organization (Goldberg, 1970[a]).

When the Self avoids new and complex situations in order to maximize certainty of outcome, it experiences itself as having little or no freedom of choice over its behavior. This experience of enervation is rationalized to justify further attempts to minimize choice. In other words, the more freedom the Self attributes to its actions, the more uncertainty it faces in choosing alternatives. But if the Self assumes that it has little or no choice, it risks little by not actively choosing from among uncertain possibilities. If it chooses a customary response in any given situation, it can expect with some certainty that what happened in the past will happen again.

The need to reduce freedom of choice results, understandably, in the loss of possibility for the Self to express its intentionality. To compensate for this loss, the Self may retreat into a world of wishes and fantasy in which all things seem possible without incurring risk or anxiety. In the retreat from devastating feelings of powerlessness, the will may be temporarily or even permanently suspended. Macquarrie (1967) indicates that

> ... all genuine willing must take account of *factical* possibility, that is to say, of possibility that is open in the particular situation. At no time does [the Self] stand before pure possibility. The illusion that [it] does ... can result only in an unrealistic and impractical existence in which will has been, in varying degrees, stifled and overcome by fantasy.

An inability to move out of a retreat into fantasy may lead to madness. This occurs when

> the self attempts to preserve its being, paradoxically, by avoiding being itself. It avoids being in an attempt to deal with the anxieties and dangers which threaten it, by constructing a "false self" as a "modus vivendi" to protect its "true self." In an attempt to maintain its integrity, its wholeness, it becomes a "divided self." The false self, constructed to adjust to false realities, is a willed position taken in order to be at all. But this strategy, again paradoxically, defeats itself, because in the defensive maneuver invented for survival, the self descends into nonbeing.... Rather than *willing* to be the self that it is, the self *wills* to construct itself. [Sugarman, 1974]

The Self remains immobilized until it is able to seize upon a direction to assert itself in the world. Directionality requires both spatial and temporal possibility, but we need discuss only the temporal dimension at this point. Piaget's concept of "decentration of perception" is helpful in understanding how the Self frees itself from a sense of immobilized will by committing itself to a temporal direction. The will frees itself

> by a double act of reversibility: either I recall the past, or I anticipate the future. I recall the past, that is to say that I am engaged, that the work has to be finished and I have to do my work. Or, on the contrary, I anticipate the future, I anticipate the satisfaction that this work will give me when accomplished, what I am going to feel when I will no longer be engaged in this task which is not particularly pleasant to me. Therefore, the act of will consists here simply in relying upon a decentration, upon something which is exactly analogous to the reversibility of the intellectual operation and which consists in subordinating the actual value, the desire, to a larger scale of

values, the value of the engagement that I have undertaken, the value of the work. From the moment that I react according to my ordinary scale of values, from the moment that I include my actual desire in the permanent scale of values, the conflict is resolved.... [Piaget, 1962]

3. *The willingness to engage possibility.* Conceptualizations of volition (when last found in textbooks of psychology) viewed will as the force of moral intellect. It operated more or less in the following stages: First, the intellect was alerted and oriented by education to recognize and distinguish moral from less moral courses of action. Second, the character of the personality (as developed through religious and moral discipline) exhorted the Self to want to follow the most virtuous path. Third, the Self would then free energy, by suppressing lesser and distracting pursuits, to follow the moral course of action.

In this paradigm, will was regarded as blind, a powerful energy force (will power) set free by moral rectitude when a virtuous objective was recognized. Pursuit of willed endeavor was on all-or-nothing effort. "My country right or wrong" and "California or bust" are emotional exhortations that derive from this economic notion of will. In this endeavor, there were no alternatives, compromises, or substitutes.

Modern psychology and psychiatry, to the extent they consider the concept of will, have abandoned the notion of will as a moral and intellectual faculty operating on an all-or-nothing principle. According to May (1974), psychoanalysis came into being largely because of the failure of will to accomplish the moral and intellectual requirements of the Victorian personality. Freud uncovered the Victorian concept of will as a "web of rationalizations and self-deceit" used in the service of repression. The Victorian personality, in short, tried to deny all irrational tendencies and infantile wishes that were unacceptable to its self-image as mature and responsible. Regarding will as powerless in the dialectical struggle between instinct and superego prohibitions, psychoanalytic investigators attempted to demonstrate that we are often deceived about what we will. Some theorists have, of course, argued that, in fact, we do not will at all but simply act out forces beyond our awareness and control. In short, the notion of will as an especially powerful mental faculty that competes with other powerful but baser faculties in choosing between moral absolutes has been dismissed as simplistic and inaccurate.

Recent writers on the concept of will—such as Farber (1968), Frankl (1969), May (1974), and Arieti (1975)—have sought to demonstrate the close relationship of will to the concepts of meaning, purpose, and human growth. These theorists have related the function of will to the intentionality of the Self. They have been influenced by the ideas of Martin Heidegger (1962), who believed that will manifests itself when a person commits himself to a chosen possibility. Will has come to represent the stance and the attitude of the Self in directing itself into the world. It is no longer regarded as a mental faculty in competition with other psychological functions of the Self, but as a term to describe a series of integrated psychological functions.

May, Farber, and Frankl describe a concept of assertive will, but this is not a force that the Self asserts upon the world in opposition to other Selves. It is, rather, an expression of the Self's attempt to establish a meaningful rapport with other Selves. Previous notions that regarded will as an autonomous, all-or-nothing force neglected a vital function of will: an assertion of the Self's need to define and establish itself in each situation it encounters.

As an entity that seeks to express its being, the Self requires dialogue with other Selves in order to reveal its intentionality to itself. When it addresses interpretations by other Selves that are inaccurate, constricting, or inauthentic definitions of what the Self intends for itself, the Self is able to affirm itself in a purposive way. These encounters also address the spatial requirements for the liberation of will referred to earlier. As the embodied representation of personality, Self cannot exist meaningfully if it relates only to itself (Sartre, 1956; Husserl, 1964). Its meaningfulness is transactional, relating in time and place with other Selves.

The developmental task in the third phase requires the Self to overcome its discouragement and despair about achieving open and caring dialogue with other Selves. In this way it gains the opportunity of expressing the experience of its own existence. Will is socially created through the Self's interactions with other Selves. Without social validation of its possibilities, will as an active agent is compelled to force itself into the world on its own. This endeavor is called "willfulness"—an attempt to will what cannot be willed through solitary effort. It is a pathology of will by which the Self experiences an immediate need to get something done without directing this intent toward realistic possibility. The Self experiences

> the ever-widening split between will and the impossible object of the will. As the split widens, the bondage between the will and its object grows, so that one is compelled to pursue what seems to wither or altogether vanish in the face of such pursuit. [Farber, 1968]

As discussed above, it is the Self that directs the will as it expresses its own intentionality. Clinically, we discover that if the Self is not given social validation for seeking possibility, it experiences a feeling that it does not deserve freedom of choice. The resolution of the developmental task comes by addressing the constricting postures that the Self takes in relation to other Selves. The Self's first acts of will are simultaneously an inhibition of its instinctual tendencies and a compliance with the demands of other Selves.

When it becomes socialized, the act of will loses the primitive mechanisms of a purely physiologic activity and instead becomes regulated by the Self's relationships to others (Arieti, 1961).

The quality of these relationships mediates the freedom that the Self experiences in expressing itself. Imbalanced relationships limit the Self's experience and expression of its intentionality. Clinically, we observe patients who have difficulty experiencing freedom of will engage in inequitable (overly dependent or overly solicitous) relationships with others. As a therapist I have employed a dialogue called a "basic emotional communication" to free each Self in an interpersonal encounter so that it can openly explore its intentionality with another. This approach is discussed in Appendix D of this book.

4. *The willingness to decide and act on possibility.* Freedom, says May (1977), "is most clearly shown in the human capacity to ask questions. Every question implies that there is more than one answer, otherwise it would not be asked." The developmental task of the fourth phase requires the Self to convert its questions about its own possibilities into action. It can do this only by turning to experiential curiosity and away from scientific and intellectual "evidence" of the powerlessness of will, which results in the feeling that even if the Self exerted itself, this would not make any appreciable impact on the world. Resolution of the developmental task is achieved by articulating and acting on the experiential question, "What if I act *as if I do have freedom* to choose among possibilities and when I do the course of action will be authenticated to becoming the person I seek to be?"

In acting on this existential concern, several important psychological processes become redirected in the Self. The Self begins to value possibility more than it does certainty. It seeks out anxious and uncertain possibilities, rather than avoiding them; in so doing, it frees itself of the deceptive security that it imposed on itself in limiting its awareness of possibility.

This recognition has the tendency to dilute and retract counter-willful mechanisms, and to shear away the quasi-security that has masked and long resisted enactment of attempts at validation of the Self's most deeply ingrained beliefs. Often this quasi-security has been a way of "least effort," a view of the world as fixed and stable, unamenable to change without the rue and trepidation of tremendous repercussions if the Self dare say "nay" to the apparent "nature of things."

In preferring possibility to certainty, the Self becomes aware of the greater complexity inherent in highly ambiguous situations. At the same time, it experiences a greater willingness to differentiate among these possibilities. The more it can do this, the more freedom the Self has to depart from habitual and conventional approaches to situations and to formulate novel expressions of its own identity in the world. These novel approaches are actually creative endeavors, as they find new unities in the variety of nature. This idea connects the concept of free will with that of determinism. These new unities and ways of being are the way they must be as they are causally connected with past events. Yet they are unique, for they did not occur as a possibility until the Self took the risk of willing possibility to that of certainty. The greater the risk, the greater the possibility. In a way, then, choices are not so much presented to us as we present choices to a world that just "is." While events shape men, men can similarly shape events.

When it responds to increased dimensions of experience, the Self finds a unity between things that were not previously thought to be alike, giving the Self a sense of richness and understanding—intrinsically pleasurable and worth the risk of discomfort inherent in confronting new situations. There comes to the attention of the Self a surge of vitality and conviction that enables it to commit itself to a particular possibility, that is, to act.

The Self that has achieved this posture is willing to risk aloneness and possible estrangement of other Selves when it expresses itself in novel ways that might be undesirable or uncomfortable to others. The Self realizes that its choices are its alone to make. No one can choose for another, although some may subtly arrange to act for others—as their guardians or as their tormentors. In permitting another to act for it, the Self chooses to negate some part of its being, to suppress the expression of that part as being too meaningless or too troublesome to be recognized. The moment a Self becomes conscious of itself, it is forced to bear the awesome responsibility of having to choose itself. The Self becomes what it seeks to be only through a full acceptance of the responsibility of choosing for itself (Goldberg, 1973).

Like Spinoza, May (1977) has indicated that freedom is the awareness of determinism. May writes:

> Freedom and determinism give birth to each other. Every advance in freedom gives birth to a new determinism, and every new determinism gives birth in turn to new freedom . . . . By refusing to accept either determinism or freedom, we diminish ourselves. Without determinism and the predictability that goes with it, we have *anarchy*. Without freedom, and the exuberance that goes with it, we have *apathy*.

In concluding this chapter I would like to agree with Martin Buber that, above all else, what psychology and psychiatry need most for their future development is a psychology of will. In this chapter I have tried to take a step in this direction.

A Theory of Emotions— Emotionality as the Expression of the Self's Intentionality

"Every true man . . . lives so as to give a meaning and a value of his own to life."
—Luigi Pirandello

There is currently a need in the behavioral sciences[1] to develop a comprehensive theory of human emotions[2] and to integrate this theory with existing knowledge of cognition, volition, and manifest activity. Heretofore, the psychotherapeutic arts, in an endeavor to become sciences, have had considerable difficulty reconciling the nature of human emotions, with their spontaneous and mercurial manifestations, within a deterministic system. As a result, the various scientific explanations of emotions have generally attempted to circumvent the unpredictability of human emotions by explaining away emotions as an epiphenomenon (for example, in James's system, the affects of neurological processes; in Freud's various theories, uncathexied libidinous energy; in Skinner's conceptualizations, stimulus responses to bodily or environmental forces).

Prevailing notions in behavioral science about the nature and manifestation of emotion have poorly served mankind. Personality theory is deficient without a unifying concept, like emotionality, which takes human intent and purpose into account. Due to reductionistic conceptualization in the behavioral sciences, emotionality has lost its indispensable function as a guide for directing the individual's existence [Goldberg, in press]. Rollo May (1974) traces the repudiation of emotionality as purposive human activity to shifts in scientific reasoning in the twentieth century:

> When William James says, "Feeling is everything," he means not that there is nothing *more* than feeling, but that everything starts there. Feeling commits one, ties one to the object, and ensures action. But in the decades after James made this "existential" statement, feeling became demoted and was disparaged as merely subjective. Reason or, more accurately, technical reason was the guide to the way issues were to be settled. We said "I feel" as a synonym for "I vaguely believe" when we didn't know—little realizing that we cannot *know* except as we feel. [P. 300]

Contemporary Ontological Malaise

We no longer regard the manifestation of emotion as a unifying and meaning-endowing human capacity—indeed, the Self's *raison d'état*. And yet, in closely examining human experience, we inevitably discover that the evocation of deeply encountered feeling fosters the processes and provides the direction toward which we aspire as purposive beings. Emotions are essential to human endeavor. When we are in contact with our emotions, we have an unswaying gauge of what we seek from our existence (Goldberg, 1973). This deficiency of manifested emotionality has serious implications for the dilemma of modern man. Increasingly, as clinicians, we find that our clients, who exist without the exchange of deeply experienced and meaningful sentiments with other Selves, come to realize that their values are vacuous, their pursuits bereft of happiness, and their endeavors lacking of direction and purpose. Without the inescapable immediacy and vividness of human emotionality, the individual feels that he is ailing, possessed by a sickness that is neither physical nor emotional, but rather a malaise of spirit, a sickness of alienation, no less epidemic and socially contagious despite the absence of an organic etiology. These persons find themselves separated not only from other Selves but estranged from themselves as well (Goldberg, 1977[a]).

Individuals possessed by ontological malaise may attempt psychotherapeutic treatment. More frequently than ever before, they languish in these situations more frustrated and disillusioned than when they entered. Bernstein (1972) attributes a considerable number of treatment failures to a passionless encounter between therapist and client. The enervation of thera-peutic alliance, he argues, stems from a prohibition against compassionate behavior on the therapists part, derived from misapplications of Freud's in-tent in cautioning against countertransferential reaction in the analyst and from Freud's recommendation of an abstinence rule for the analysand.

Emotion as Reaction

One of the most common assumptions about emotions is that a feel-ing-state is a subjective push from within the person which sets the Self into motion. May (1974) has described this ubiquitously accepted model as

> a kind of glandular hydraulis—we have an inner secretion of adrenalin and need to let off our anger, or gonadal excitement and find a sexual object. [P. 89]

In regarding emotion as a reactive mechanism, rather than a human ac-tion with a prescriptive intent, epistemological attempts to recognize the Self's capacity for purposive action are dismissed by behavioral scientists as rationalizations about unknown behavioral precursors. The jettison of emo-tionality as prescriptive statement is unfortunate. I submit that reactive theories of emotion are both philosophically unproductive and scientifically unsound. I also object to the repudiation of purposive human emotion on pragmatic grounds. Scientific discussion about the role of emotion has self-fulfilling societal implications. Formerly, theological and natural-science concepts were regarded as relevant for explaining human nature. At the present, behavioral-science explanations have higher credibility among the general populace. As with the concept of will discussed in the last chapter, the attitudes of behavioral scientists about the function of emotionality serve as guidelines for others. Both individuals and social institutions em-ploy these models to define the range of possibility within which the indi-vidual has the freedom to be responsible for his own actions (Goldberg, 1977[b]).

The Quest for Meaning

The recurring theme of human existence is the Self's striving for per-sonal identity, significance, and unification. In short, man craves a sense of meaning for his existence (Goldberg, 1973). Meaning is derived from our passions. Our passions induce us to become involved in our existence. Why else would we continue to struggle with "the slings and arrows of outrageous fortunes," other than in the fervent desire to participate in the full enrichment of our passions!

It is our passions that give our struggles and our triumphs—whether transitory or more enduring—a sense of meaning. As we sow our passions, so we reap our destiny. If we invest ourselves in passionless pursuits, we are entrusting our lives to fate and the intentions of external agents. In so doing, we lose mastery over our lives and, as a consequence, experience hopelessness or indifference toward our destiny. Without an emotionally imbued sense of purpose, life is experienced as unbearably frightening and unfathomly barren. Rarely has this existential dread been described more harrowly than by the French philosopher Blaise Pascal (1946), in depicting man as the feeblest reed in nature:

> When I consider the brief span of my life, swallowed up in eternity before and behind it, the small space that I fill, or even see, engulfed in the infinite immensity of spaces which I know not, and which know not me, I am afraid, and wonder to see myself here rather than there; for there is no reason why I should be here rather than there, now rather than then.... [P. 35]

The purpose of this chapter is to explore the development of a sense of purpose and mastery of our emotions so that we need not be forever a captive of the existential dread so poignantly described by Pascal. The theme I will be arguing is that passion and commitment are the only meaningful antidotes to our hopelessness and despair. Without the arousal of passion and the commitment to an identifiable set of values, Self-understanding, however persistently pursued, does not enable the Self to meaningfully participate with other objects-in-the-world.

Human Intentionality

Nietzsche and Kierkegaard long ago exhorted the psychologist to return to intuition in seeking truth and ontological direction for the individual's existence, a turning back to the vitality of the resurrected life forces. The psychologist's overemphasis on rationality and intellectual understanding were for Nietzsche antilife—a caution against the direct experience of life. Reason, he argued, never gives us immediate knowledge. At best, reason tenders a vicarious approximation to life—the role of the unrisking observer. Nietzsche and Kierkegaard were objecting to a societal view of passion as a pastime to enjoy while on holiday, or as a distraction and inter-ference with rational, task-oriented endeavors. This view has continued to our day and, we know from clinical experience, has fostered a pervasive sense of detachment from ourselves and others—an inability to be aware of one's own intentions, to make commitments, or to perform constructive ac-tions.

A similar theme has been raised recently by the British playwright, Pe-ter Shaffer. In *Equus,* a controversial drama about modern psychiatry, Shaf-fer proclaims that modern society typically produces uninspired people who, in fearing their emotions, lack a commitment to themselves and others. He indicts psychiatry for colluding in this dehumanizing process. Dr. Martin Dysart, the psychiatrist-protagonist of the play, derides the psychological practice he serves. Passion, he indicates, is indispensable to life. What can psychiatry offer in its·place? Nonetheless, Dysart is unable or unwilling to redefine his psychological role. As a representative of psychiatry he remains entombed in an obsessive prison, willing only to observe and vicariously identify with the passions of his "demented" patient.

Is Shaffer correct? Have the behavioral sciences lost the name of action in dealing with alienation and ontological malaise? I believe that a strong case can be made for the affirmative. Therefore, I strongly disagree with those theatre critics and psychotherapists who have condemned Shaffer's play as nothing more than "a trite psychiatric case history." I believe that Shaffer is posing questions that psychiatry must respond to if it is to survive as a viable modality for dealing with the human condition. At its core, Shaffer's play questions the role of human intentionality in psychiatry.

Human intentionality has to do with the Self's attempt to define its place in-the-world. It is a point of view established to dispel the notion that personality can be defined and understood in terms of what it "is" (an es-sentialistic position), rather than what the Self does (an existential posi-tion). Behavioral scientists have failed to relate emotionality to the other be-havioral activities of the personality, because they have assumed that the Self resides as an inner realm "within" the person, to be revealed by inter-pretative insights and introspection. The notion of intentionality posits, in contrast, that the Self exists as an object-in-the-world, which creates mean-ing for itself by its passionate involvement in the relations and events of the world. The various projections that the Self casts of itself on the world con-sist of attitudes and intents of how the Self seeks to be known. Personality must, therefore, be defined within the context of the Self and its intended objects. This is to say, what the Self does defines it. There is nothing beyond the nature of the act as the real motive or impetus for the Self's involvement with other objects. Our identity consists of the composite of specific acts the Self takes toward other Selves and the meaning with which it imbues these acts (Wheelis, 1970). We come to know who we are, and by implication what we intend, by examining how we act; that is to say, what we concretely do in the situations and relations in which we find ourselves. Our feelings are lucid and meaningful only in terms of our actions, rather than our declarations or inferred repressed motives. In short, emotions are expressions of the Self's intentionality in addressing its concerns and purposes in being-in-the-world. In Ofman's (1976) words:

> Emotions are special ways of getting what we want, of confirming and illustrating who we are. [P. 79]

A Rational for Understanding Human Intentionality

The problem intentionality poses for the healing arts is that to the extent that the Self's intentionality remains inaccessible to direct experience, the Self cannot get into itself and is thus forced to avoid itself. This avoidance is a denial of both the desire and the possibility of the freedom of the Self to express itself-in-the-world. Rollo May (1974) points to the direction I will follow, in trying to delineate a rationale for enabling the behavioral scientist to recognize paths the Self may follow in realizing its own intentionality, when he indicates that

> ... emotions are not just a push from the rear but a *pointing toward* something, an impetus for forming something, a call to mold the situation. Feelings are not just a chance state of moment, but a pointing toward the *future,* a way I *want* something to be. Except in the most severe pathology, feelings always occur in a personal field, an experience of one's Self as personal and an imagining of others even if no one else is literally present. [P. 90]

May is describing emotionality as a prescription—a statement of meaning-directed behavior that needs to be given voice and understood within the context of the individual as a purposive being who invents (builds) reality in consensus with other Selves. This theme is also apparent in the recent writing of Robert C. Solomon. Solomon (1977) argues that emotionality does not exist as a reality separate from the external world of objects and events, but rather serves to give meaning and value to our objective reality.

> Our passions—our emotions, moods, and desires—define us, our Selves, and the world we live in. [Solomon, 1977; p. xviii]

Both May and Solomon are contending that the external world merely "is," that is, the external world consists of physical properties that have no inherent meaning or value. Value and meaning are personal evaluations. The Self invests the external world with meaning by projecting its intentions onto the world through the expression of its passions. To illustrate: A patient became aware that a certain woman of his acquaintance might call him. He initially was uncertain about how he should behave during the prospective conversation. In short, he was not sure what he wanted from her. He became aware—by role-playing in his head—that if he expressed to her a particular feeling (sharing with her some unsettling personal issues), she would respond in a particular way (she would indicate her concern). Most importantly, however, he realized that if she expressed concern about his agitation, he would feel committed to maintain his sad demeanor and would, in fact, create external conditions to foster his mood. In a word, in choosing, however unwittingly, to feel a certain way, each of us brings about particular responses from others and experiences a commitment to define and maintain himself in this mood.

The Self is an evaluative entity—its sense of itself is derived from the sum total of evaluations of the relations in which the Self enters, or from which the Self withholds itself. The sense of Self, again, is derived from what the Self does—its acts and the value and the meaning the Self attributes to these acts. Acts and relations, in themselves, are neutral. They are the "facts" of the external world. The meaning accruing to these facts is derived from the judgments and, the concomitant, emotionality projected by the Self onto its activities. Consequently, if the Self *acts as if* what the Self is doing is authentic to its intentionality, the Self experiences its activities and its relations-in-the-world to be meaningful. As a result, the sense of Self is accentuated; that is, experienced with a heightened sense of unity with the world—a feeling of being in concert with the world.

This rationale has implications for what has been referred to as "inappropriate" or "disordered" behavior. The Self's response to a given situation is intentionally never "inappropriate" (for example, laughing in a "serious" situation). Rather, the situation as defined by the other objects involved is incongruous with how the Self intends to present itself and to experience itself-in-the-world. By acting "inappropriately," the Self is trying to inform itself and other Selves that the situation, as it is being defined and reacted to, needs to be modified. The Self that regards the world as having objective meaning and value reverses its ontological prerequisite and becomes a reactive agent. Avoidance of Self is implied in the reactive stance. The Self avoids itself by ignoring the objects of its consciousness. The Self remains passive when it holds itself from projecting its intentions into the world, because the objects of its awareness present the Self with no external or universal meaningfulness. Ignoring the facts (objects) of the Self's awareness depletes possibility, leaving the Self with a diminished or even depleted sense of its possibilities for being-in-the-world. Boredom, for example then, is ignoring what the Self is aware of, for example, possibility for relationship and sharing with other Selves, until nothing is left in consciousness with which to be engaged. The devastating existential experiences of alienation, dread, and nonbeing come from the Self remaining entrenched in itself as a reactive agent—with a diminished sense of possibility of becoming personally involved with oneself and other objects.

The Development of Human Meaning[4]

Both the conditions that facilitate and those that inhibit the development of a sense of meaningfulness have practical consequences for the practitioner. As a therapist I have become increasingly aware of various interferences, as well as task requirements in the development of my clients' ability and willingness to derive meaning from their existence. I will delineate the development of meaning in terms of five phases of the evolution of Self. (Since we all experience emotion, the point is not how we develop feelings, but rather how the ways of experiencing emotion we all incur develop into a sense of purpose for our being-in-the-world). Each of the phases to be described requires a definitive developmental task, as the Self evolves from the primitive state of emotionality as an adaptive (reactive) entity to the condition of the Self as a purposive entity, who strategizes in constituting itself-in-the-world.

1. The Sensory Self.

In its most primitive state of development, emotions happen to the Self in reaction to pleasant or aversive events in which the Self finds itself thrust. The Self in its primitive state finds itself, as if looking at itself as an object, as happy, sad, or whatever. When emotionality occurs, it is generally ebullient. Its moods are abrupt and often extreme. But, typically, the Self's demeanor is one of indifference or subtle discomfort. The developmental task in the first phase is to become aware of possibility. To do this, the Self must first examine the assumptions it makes about presenting itself-in-the-world.

In this writer's exploration of the unquestioned assumption of behavioral scientists that they are experts in regard to the realities of other Selves, I have returned to Schopenhauer's simple and profound opening statement to his *The World As Will And Idea* (1966). He states, "The world is my representation (idea)." Schopenhauer is implying that the world simply "is." How I experience the world consists of my assumptions about the world, having little or nothing to do with how the world really is (Goldberg, 1978[a]). Watts (1961) examines this notion when he indicates that

> some discussions of liberation suggest that what is involved is not so much objective as subjective release from the physical world. In other words, it is assumed that our normal perception of the spatially and temporally extended world, and of the sense organs which transact with it, is a type of hypnotic illusion, and that anyone who acquired perfect concentration can see for himself that the spatiotemporal world is nothing but imagination. [P. 62]

Schopenhauer's statement leads to the realization that no person can actually be an expert in regard to objective reality, much less the idiosyncratic realities of other Selves. This is as true for the scientist or therapist as for his subject or client. Nonetheless, personal responsibility is predicated upon the Self's commitment to withstand varying degrees of discomfort and risk in questioning the validity of its assumptions about what it is to exist as a Self and move around in the world, as the Self constitutes that world.

The endeavor to become aware of possibility requires that the Self reorient itself toward its own bodily being. As the Self becomes appreciative of its assumptions, it discerns how these assumptions induce postures—physically, psychologically, and spiritually. These postures predicate how the Self experiences its being-in-the-world. To contact its internal needs, the Self must transcend these postures by closing off from its own typical undifferentiation and fusion with other Selves and get into itself. To experience its own natural bodily rhythm, unfettered by the need for socially structured expression, the Self must turn away from objects-in-the-world for intending. When feeling bodily sensation—whether pleasant, anxious, fearful, or whatever—the Self turns away from seeking objects for fantasized or active engagement. The Self turns into itself by focusing on its bodily sensations, emptying its consciousness of thoughts and instead centering on internal sensations, allowing its soma to become accessible to its own energies.

Human purpose has to do with the struggle with ambivalence and pain. The Self must push into the murky, veiled emptiness and loneliness hidden within, and stay persistently with these uncomfortable and aversive sensations. To feel deeply, as in pain, is to become aware that I hurt because I *care*. The Self accentuates its caring by making a moment-to-moment decision to endure and to do something with its experience; that is to say, not to ignore, neglect or suppress what it is feeling. The Self takes an attitude toward living for the struggle—to struggle another day is to seek possibility for another day! This caring through pain has been movingly expressed by the poetess, Anne Sexton:

> Creative people must not avoid the pain that they get dealt. I say to myself, sometimes repeatedly, "I've got to get the hell out of this hurt"—But, no. Hurt must be examined like a plague. [Sexton and Ames, 1977]

Victor Frankl (1964) describes a similar realization in bearing what was experienced by some as intolerable suffering in the concentration camps: To live is to suffer, to survive is to find meaning in the suffering.

> If there is a meaning in life at all, then there must be a meaning in suffering. Suffering is an ineradicable part of life—without suffering—life cannot be complete. [P. 106]

However, as Allport [1964] adds:

> No man can tell another what this purpose is. Each must find out for himself, and must accept the responsibility that his answer prescribes. If he succeeds he will continue to grow in spite of all indignities. Frankl is fond of quoting Nietzsche, "He who has a *why* to live can bear almost any *how*." [P. xiii]

Suffering is derived from our primitive awareness and struggle to affirm our own individuality in an indifferent and alien world (Groddeck, 1977). Ambivalence and pain are the raw ingredients with which we are confronted in attempting to learn about the quality of the Self and the world in which we have been thrust. It is only in the doing, in the active struggle to articulate our sense of being in an unknown world that meaning is given birth. Ofman (1976) describes what I refer to as "becoming aware of possibility" as

> a pointing toward something outside itself—an object or an event—and always implies an attitude, a project, or an *intention*. It is in this way that intentionality gives meaningful context to consciousness. . . . Intentionality is a dialectic relationship within which meaning originates—it is an interaction through which a person transforms the brute material of his surroundings into his "situation." Man, then, is always in a situation. [P. 32]

2. The Courageous Self.

The developmental task in the second phase of Self is for the Self to turn toward possibility—that is to say, for the Self to act upon the belief that possibility comes into being when the Self dares to go beyond that toward which it has typically confined itself. To do this the Self must risk alienation and aloneness in going beyond its *standing out* from among others—its willingness to define itself differently than other Selves define it. Most of our existence is conducted habitually, without the awareness of strong emotion or a sense of meaningfulness. Most of our daily roles and relationships are designed to deny and buffer us from our aloneness and our existential fate–our dread of nonbeing (Goldberg, 1975[b]). To experience a sense of meaning requires standing out from the undifferentiated, unemotional others. To stand out, to act as one's own agent, the Self must constantly get into itself. It must constantly confront its existential anxiety and dread. It must, in short, be aware at all times of its impotence, of its fears, and its failures. May (1974) has described modern man in this regard as seeking

> virtue without trying, sex without risk, wisdom without struggle, luxury without effort–all provided that they agree to settle for love without passion.... [P. 70]

It is obvious that where possibility is sought, risks are inherent and certainty unassured. This is because human purpose is only meaningful to an *existent*–someone who is finite and will someday cease to be. An individual gains purpose by seriously grappling with his finiteness and his mortality. Without appreciating the meaning of time in human existence, the individual's attempts at a meaningful definition of himself as a finite, purposive-seeking being are doomed to futility. The crux of our existential dilemma is that, whereas the use and structuring of time are essential in seeking meaning in human existence, the fear of contaminating and dissipating our precious time by probing the dimensions of temporality has led to our pervasive disuse and denial of time. To ignore the individual's phenomenological experience of time, that is, how he uses and structures his existence, however, is to deal with artifacts of human experience oblique to the mercurial uncertainty of "lived" existence. Thus, the Self must find a means of indulging itself in the *immediacy* of its existence (Goldberg, 1977[a]). The Self comes to this indulgence by valuing possibility. Finding meaning in the Self's experience is initially made possible not by knowledge but by faith. The psychological freedom we seek is derived from the experience that excising our belief in psychological freedom enables us to act, rather than to remain passive (Goldberg, 1977[b]). In facing up to the legitimacy of its intentionality, the Self redirects its relationship with the world; in facing up to being as it intends, the Self creates possibility for the expression of its being as real possibility.

The reader might well ask at this junction where does the desire to give purpose to one's life emanate from–how does the Self come to choose this option? Perhaps too much attention in our day has been placed on freedom, which is seen as a throwing off of the condition in which we find ourselves, as if we could become someone or something else. It should be apparent that we can only become what we have intended for ourselves and what we have not yet become aware of and realized. What we require to give meaning to our lives is not escape to some abstract state of freedom, but rather courage, the *areté* of the ancient Greeks, for fulfilling and bearing with dignity and fortitude what we are. Pindar exhorts us: "Become what you are!"

The Self cannot escape itself. Since it can only be what it has intended for itself, the Self must will what it cannot escape. The Self could have chosen another direction only if it were another Self. What is real is what affects me. I invent my world by being open to respond and permitting myself to be affected by the world. In opening myself to the world and letting myself be affected by the world, I cannot avoid the realization of the illusion of my most fervent hopes and aspirations. This disillusionment, which evokes pain and despair, is replete with desire. The hurt, the elation, whatever I experience from my previous acts and the events in which I was involved, enable me to choose what I could not have chosen without realizing my desires. This is to say, the Self can only choose from within the context of its own experience. Having experienced and fulfilled the developmental needs of its intending, the Self can then evolve.

To some extent, however, in every moment of our lives, clearly in states of agitated emotion, we wrestle with assuaging our desires—and the pain and despair borne—with the security of cognitive certainty. We at once "know everything," but we struggle to try to figure out by concepts and words what we have already experienced emotionally. In an instant, we sense the being of the other, we appreciate at once our feelings about the other and what we seek from him. But we are aware that to desire is to experience fear—we fear that we will never achieve what we most fervently desire. In defense against disillusionment, we tell ourselves that we don't really know what we want. A patient who was a struggling writer found himself unable to write after encountering a former girlfriend who had rejected him about a year prior. His association to the event was that he didn't want to be a failure like his father, who always claimed to know what he wanted but avoided going after it because he needed financial and emotional security. In this patient's mind, if he didn't know what he wanted he couldn't be regarded as a coward. If he consciously admitted what he wanted, he feared he would prove to be a failure like his father. Existentially, however, not to let oneself know desire is to remain stuck—reactively entrenched. To admit desire is to experience fear, but the Self can move even if it does so with trepidation.

The last of human freedom Frankl (1964) describes with inescapable conviction from his concentration camp experience, is the ability "to choose one's attitude in a given set of circumstances, to choose one's own way" (p. 104). Frankl tells us that the prisoners were only average men, but some, at least by choosing to be "worthy of their suffering," proved the self's capacity to rise above its outward fate.

Courage is a concept assiduously avoided by behavioral scientists in explaining human behavior. To the behavioral scientist, no doubt, courage is a term best left with athletes, soldiers, and true believers. It is not a construct which may be readily accounted for in deterministic terms. To the behavioral scientist, it smacks of ascribing enviable characteristics to behaviors that would have inevitably occurred without the imposition of the hypothesized emotion which has been appellated "courage." As such, courage may be dismissed as an epiphenomenon and discarded with the other remnants of human purpose and intention. For the imputation of the concept of courage is not actually necessary for accounting for human action. But without the attribution of courage, human dignity and passion become quickly dismantled.

Nietzsche recognized that so much of our technical society was devoted to making life easy that modern man has lost his human dignity in facing up to the painful issues of human existence. Without courage, modern man will continue to avert these ontological concerns. In staying courageously with my pain and my despair, I sense my caring—my passion to push through the indifference and the stolidness of my world. To care courageously necessitates a *revolt* against my world as it is. Camus, as Wilson (1963) indicates

> recommended rebellion as the proper philosophical stance toward life . . . rebellion against indignity, against the impotent and irrational and unmanly. [P. 2]

Why is revolt necessary? Caring isn't enough for deriving meaning in my life. Meaning is directed, has a sense of purpose. It is caring which creates possibility in terms of the objects that comprise the contents of my consciousness. But it is the rebellion of my Self from the confines of the strictures and guidelines imposed by other Selves which gives me direction. In the sentiments of Nicholas Berdyaev (1955), any "answer" the world can offer us will not be a stable one or a final reality, because the desire to know the world has always been accompanied by the desire to alter the world. In order to know and alter the world, a man must accept the role of rebel. Only in the act of rebellion can a man create his own meaning. Contrary to the views of some, the rebel is not in search of an identity. It is only at the point he recognizes "what he is," or more properly, *"what he wills to become,"* that a man rebels. As a rebel the courageous Self cries out against the conditions imposing upon his human condition. He claims that there are limits to the infringements that others may impose upon his condition. He becomes at some point so impatient with the forces imposing upon him that he can hold back no longer and breaks "the chains of tolerance and indifference" to which he has permitted himself to become reconciled. He insists that he is aware that some other, more preferable existence, is possible, and he is willing to chance any repercussions to achieve it. The world the courageous Self wishes to live in is a world he has made for himself. He is rebelling against the prefabricated, stolid world into which he has found himself thrust.

Granted, there are aversive "acting out" forms of rebellion. This is not what I mean in this context. Camus (1960) comes closest to what I mean in defining a rebel as a man who says "No," but whose refusal does not imply a renunciation. He is also a man who says "Yes" to some areas of his life, because he has come to identify some set of attitudes and beliefs about himself and the world as crucial to the maintenance of his existence. The rebel says, "I cannot accept the old values. I must create my own!"

> In every act of rebellion, the rebel simultaneously experiences a feeling of revulsion at the infringements of his rights and a complete and spontaneous loyalty to another aspect of himself. Thus he implicitly brings into play a standard of values so far from being gratuitous that he is prepared to support it no matter what the risks. Up until this point he has at least remained silent and has abandoned himself to the form of despair in which a condition is accepted even though it is considered unjust. To remain silent is to give the impression that one has no opinion, that one wants nothing.... But from the moment that the rebel finds his voice—even though he says nothing but "no"—he begins to desire and judge ... suddenly he turns and faces himself. He opposes what is preferable to what is not. Not every value entails rebellion but every act of rebellion tacitly invokes a value. [Camus, 1960; pp. 13–14]

Rebellion has the propensity of acting upon the whole man. It tears away the complacency and quasi-security from the Self that have masked and long resisted insight into the Self's most deeply ingrained beliefs. Often the quasi-security has been a way of least effort. A view of the world as fixed and stable, unamenable to change without the rue and trepidation of strenuous repercussions if the Self dare say "Nay" to the nature of things. The courageous Self, therefore, is required to leap into uncertainty. As Kierkegaard (1954) passionately wrote: "Man in despair is unaware that his condition is despair." As passion by itself has only momentary satisfaction so, too, intellectual, scientific, and materialistic enterprises were for Kierkegaard unable to heal the break between the self and its world; only a leap of faith could accomplish this (Jones, 1969).

It is the ownership and passionate scrutiny of one's convictions—along with the awareness of the fear and uncertainty accrued—that comprise courage. There is always courage involved in acknowledging the dissonance of one's ideology and aspirations, and the condition one finds oneself-in-the-world. It is, therefore, an acknowledgment of the inevitability of one's intentions that calls upon courage. The Self must first be what it intends to be to further evolve. As clinicians, we must be aware that our clients do not change what they and/or others regard as dysfunctional aspects of themselves until they come to accept and understand themselves as they are. To do otherwise, they would be inclined to expend their energy in denying and defending themselves against what they are intending to be (Goldberg, 1970^a). Courage, then, is not admitting error, but in affirming the Self's presence in the world as best it can.

3. The Intuitive Self.

By the intuitive phase the Self has some notion of its wants and needs and has freed up its vitality by its courageous willingness to let its intentionality stand out from the other Selves around it. The Self, however, still has not affirmed its commitment to possibility. The Self has to commit its vitality (its will) to focus on a single preferred possibility in relation to other possibilities. For this to happen, the Self must go beyond its own immediate experience to grasp the relation between the world as it is presently constituted and a wish or idea of how the Self wishes to constitute itself.

Weisman (1965) in this regard indicates that

> nothing has meaning apart from its reference to something else. The concept of meaning itself usually refers to a link between a more or less abstract idea and a concrete experience. A novel or isolated event can be recognized only when it already has some meaning. [P. 37]

The developmental task in the intuitive phase requires the Self to come to understand how the Self, as it presently constitutes itself, can create the world in relationship with itself as the Self intends. This understanding, however, cannot be derived rationally or intellectually. Rationality is a shared language, a common way of interpreting and sensing the world with that of other Selves. As a rational Self, the Self returns to its former status as an undifferentiated, generalized other, unable to understand its unique promptings for constituting itself-in-the-world. The need for meaning in one's existence cannot, therefore, be reduced to a need for factual knowledge. Factual knowledge has validity only to the extent that external reality is allowed to define the Self. The need for meaning requires the experience of what the Self *risks* intending in shaping its experiences—going beyond the immediate and acting on its projections—its wishes, and fantasies. Foremost, however, it requires a *decision*. Decisions are evaluations. As we express our preferences, so we choose our loves and our hates. Our emotions expressed as preferences are commitments to maintain our being-in-the-world in specific ways. This is why Kierkegaard emphasized commitment as well as passion. His point was that the act which one becomes passionately committed to must be deliberately chosen. A person's awareness of choice, therefore, is not sufficient. He can only become that which he intends through an active commitment. To know a person I must appreciate not only what he experiences but, more importantly, what he has done to make his life more congruent with his feelings. Emotion, therefore, gets in the way of the creation of meaning when it is overvalued in and of itself. The sense of meaningfulness is derived then, not from simply the arousal of passion, but through the enjoyment of the vitality of passion in constructive action (Goldberg, 1973). Ofman (1976) has argued that

> man creates his own meaning, and every meaning involves a commitment to act. The act of inattention or repression is a knowledge of something toward which a person will not take action. Consequently, he has chosen not to "know" it. To attend to something, to take it seriously, implies a readiness to some decision about the situation. [P. 32]

To understand human intentionality is also to become aware that emotional moods are *strategies*. For example, a patient was feeling extremely depressed as long as he maintained the need for confirmation and caring from a woman with whom he wanted to be involved. He felt no way out of his despair. He felt that he must either endure the disappointment or find a way to deny the hurt. In his despair he was struck by the realization that the woman's lack of interest in the relationship was a challenge to him. This was a situation which could bring him in the direction he has previously intellectually claimed he intended. He wished to seek relationships in which he was not chosen by the woman—as typically women moved toward him—but which he sought for himself. Although the probability for establishing a relationship with this particular woman was remote, it was an opportunity to pursue what he sought to experience. The important realization for him was, that having made a commitment to direct himself toward what he intended, he felt rather differently than he had up until that moment. He experienced a sense of purpose and value in regard to the events with which he was struggling. He felt less resentful and more potent and optimistic about himself. As a result, he felt willing to experience to the hilt what was happening to him—an endeavor which was heretofore intolerable.

The feeling of affirmation of the struggle with one's own intentionality is, of course, rarely internalized by a single burst of insight. The interrelationship of meaning and agitated emotion flows like waves in difficult and complex experiences. At moments, the patient discussed above felt elated, caught up on the crest of self-awareness, at other moments denigrated and devastated by his need to pursue an object that eluded him. The intensity of the meaningfulness of the event shifted as different aspects of the situation were realized. But over time the intensity did not so much increase or decrease as the experience came to make "sense," became more integrated in terms of the person he sought to be, as he became aware of what the experience revealed of how heretofore he had been constituting himself in other relationships.

We set up emotional myths and belief systems—constructs of how we would like the world to be. We hold several competing myths about our being-in-the-world. In so doing, we may hold logically contradictory myths simultaneously. For example, we may believe that each cloud has a silver lining, as well as insist on being depressed if something untoward happens. We are taught these myths by our families and our contemporaries, but *we choose* among these myths, enfranchising those by which we wish to be ruled (Solomon, 1977). In a word, emotions hold priority, giving meaning to one emotional myth rather than another. As Ofman (1976) indicates: "We adopt or undertake an *emotional* attitude" (p.79).

In sum, the development of meaning in the intuitive stage comes from the Self answering for itself in terms of relations with others: how it wishes to live, to create, to overcome trepidation, and not fall prey to self-pity and hopelessness.

4. The Passionate Self.

As an entity that seeks to express its being, the Self requires dialogue with other Selves in order to reveal its intentionality to itself. A thing in itself can only be itself. Creating new possibilities requires a coming together of different Selves to actualize the potential of each, as well as to effect a blending of all. The Self through sharing absorbs and exchanges resources and energies with the other.

> Feelings are rightfully a way of communicating with significant people in our world, a reaching out to mold the relationship with them; they are a language by which we interpersonally construct and build. That is to say, feelings are intentional. [May, 1974; p. 90]

The developmental task in this phase is for the Self to create consensus reality with other Selves. The richness of human experience in this writer's view is derived from the creation of consensus reality with other Selves-in-the-world. How can the Self find meaning other than in an emotionally imbued encounter with other Selves, in which the Self is able to articulate and negotiate its values (intentions) with another Self! Richness of human experience is maximized to the extent that each Self is willing to openly negotiate for the realization of its intentionality for being-in-the-world. (In a recent book I have described a model for developing consensus reality [Goldberg, 1977ᵃ]; see Appendix D for a description of this model).

Articulation of consensus reality is always a risk. To move meaningfully toward others implies valuing *immediate engagement*. It involves a *letting go* to permit what the Self is experiencing at the present moment to emerge—in terms of values, wants and vulnerability—as it constitutes itself-in-the-world. This "letting go" requires a caring for oneself without the defensive-protective stance of constraining other Selves in relating to the Self. "Letting go" is the peferred stance of the passionate Self in being open to experience its avoidances, rather than seeking reassurance and certainty about its assumptions about the world. The Self receives caring from another by sharing its preferences and concerns with the other, freeing the other to relate to the Self as the other experiences the Self. "Reality" exists for the Self only by virtue of the way it relates with other Selves. Communication is, therefore, an extremely powerful vehicle. When the Self addresses interpretations by other Selves that are constricting or inauthentic definitions of what the Self intends for itself as an object-in-relationship, the Self is able to constitute itself in a purposive way.

Moreover, the observer may infer which phase the Self is in developmentally in its attempt to create meaning for itself by observing the quality of the Self's communication. The language the Self employs in referring to itself in relationship to other objects reveals the emotional sense the Self experiences in its being-in-the-world. In the first phase, the Self is more apt to make "you" statements than "I" statements. It makes frequent use of conventional, repetitive phrases, vague and loose generalizations, and rapid evocation of different meanings and poor connections between time and place of expression. Stereotypical language is employed, devoid of the Self's personal experience. To use others' words and concepts avoids the struggle and trepidation of one's own experience. In the second phase, the Self is more likely to make "I" statements and employ fewer blaming, defensive, and object-fused statements. The Self is apt to communicate a greater degree of personal experience. However, the Self is more likely to ask questions than to make definitive statements. In the third phase, the Self is less intellectual and introspective than it was in the former phase. It makes more specific statements of present desires, rather than posing questions that require excessive reflection. However, the Self when examining conflict with others may find it difficult to avoid interpretations and value judgments. In the fourth phase, the Self moves from a statement of needs to a statement of preferences. It is more willing to take interpersonal risks. It avoids giving and asking for declarations of essence. The passionate Self realizes that a person's intent serves to role-model attributes he seeks in another Self. Thus, he responds to the other as if the other *is* the person with whom he would like to be involved and as if he, himself, is the person he intends to be. When he feels the other Self has not fulfilled gratifications he seeks, he, himself, initiates the desired behaviors toward the other. In a word, the passionate Self realizes that he acts toward the other not only to evoke desired responses from the other but equally as important, to evoke desired responses in himself (Goldberg, 1977[a]).

5. The Creative Self.

Having created a direction and expressed the meaning of his being-in-the-world in concrete relations with other Selves, the Self attempts to commit itself to the perpetuation of its creative endeavors so as to shape itself in a new and more significant way. In the creative phase the emotions come into harmonious concert with the will. The expression of will requires a belief in psychological freedom (Goldberg, 1977[a]).

The creative Self alluded to here is identical to that of the fourth stage of will referred to as "the willingness to decide and act on possibility" discussed in chapter four, pages 58-59. It would be repetitious to describe this material here.

In summary, I have endeavored in this chapter to demonstrate that emotionality is more than simply a reaction to the events of the world or the evocation of hidden motives and urges. By giving priority (focusing on) the objects of the Self's awareness, these facts are given meaning, fulfilling the requirements of the passions as expressions of the Self's intentionality. In commiting the Self to act on the priorities of its intended evaluations, the Self moves from an inscrutable, reactive entity to an active, creative, and meaning providing being. Emotionality that involves intentionality involves an ontological question: "Will I allow the other (or circumstances) to define me—will I be dependent on the other's goodwill, protection, and concern to direct my existence *or* will I stand out—will I take the risk of acting purposively as my own agent in defining the direction of my existence?"

Meaning, then, is ontological direction gained by focusing on the contents of consciousness and giving priority and value to defining oneself in relation to those objects. In short, I have sought to delineate how states of salient distress derive from the Self not acting in terms of its objects-in-the-world as legitimate possibility. Consequently, the various emotional moods ensue in the Self, not from reactions to events, but as dissipating and dissuading processes derived from the fallacious assumption the Self makes about the nature of external reality (for example, the possibility of the universe presenting the Self with objective meaning). In this regard Wilson has aptly written:

Man is alive only in his struggle, only in his defiant engagement with a world he never made but with which he must live. . . . happiness is recognized in activity, not achieved as a state of being; personality is reviewed in process, not honed to a finished symmetry. [1963]

Consequently, clients need from their therapist courage, not ideas. They have knowledge but lack conviction. There is no answer to the question of life except courage *(areté)* in the face of what is. The therapist can, perhaps, best enable his client to achieve meaning by offering his personal concern—caring that the client's struggle to examine the assumptions he makes about his being-in-the-world will be worthy of him, to enable him to be as he intends, rather than the fulfillment of a metapsychological theory.

Chapter Six

Twilight of the Gods—
The Silent Conspiracy
Against Recognizing the
Therapeutic Struggle

"If you think you know what's going on, you're probably full of shit."
—a street proverb

For the past eighteen years I have been involved in research, teaching and writing about psychological processes. For the past thirteen years, I have been a psychotherapy practitioner and educator. I am on the teaching faculties of a medical school, several psychotherapy training institutes, and a teaching consultant to several psychiatric hospitals. I have been previously the director of a Comprehensive Community Mental Health Center. I have published six books and about thirty professional articles and chapters of edited books in the field of psychotherapy and mental health. I am a Fellow of the American Group Psychotherapy Association, a master instructor of their training institute, a member of their Standards and Ethics Committee, and have been the chairman for Continuing Education for Psychologists in private practice in the Maryland suburbs of Washington, D.C.

As an undergraduate student I was a philosophy major. As a practitioner and educator I have continued to be interested in the philosophical foundations of psychotherapy and the ethical concerns raised by psychotherapeutic involvement.

What I have cited above is a rather objective statement of my professional credentials. I am more concerned in this chapter with sharing with the reader my own ontological and narcissistic struggles to bring meaning into my work as a clinician. I will set the stage for this discussion with a brief parable.

Above the banal stage the puppeteers plotted. They decided to enact a story about a wooden bastard who could bleed and cry. He would espouse a colossal paradox. All those who heeded him would deny the obvious and believe the absurd. He would say unto them that the Eternal Kingdom of Meaning and Value was not of this stage, and they would reply "Yea!" He would tell them that this same kingdom was within every wooden puppet breast, and they would shake their loosely jointed bodies "Nay!"

Throughout the performance they would push back the stage, seeking the deified bastard. Yet they would be so close to him that they could not recognize him. He would be part of them, the part they deny—the natural part.

The natural part, the craftsman never need fashion into his wooden man. It is a part with which the puppet becomes spontaneously inculcated at the very instant the audience forgets the stage and believes that it is witnessing the struggles of real men. So it is with the Self!

I experienced little or no meaning in my life for many years as I practiced psychotherapy. I sensed that I was dying—far faster than I wished, slower than I cared. I found my life almost entirely involved with my work as a psychotherapist, theoretician, and educator. I realized that I spent more time with my clients and students than I did with others. I experienced myself as a more concerned therapist than I was a caring person outside of therapy with nonclients or toward myself. I felt little satisfaction in my marriage and im my social life. My wife was also a therapist. This was a cause of considerable friction between us. Most of the satisfactions in my life came from my clinical work. I recognized in myself, with no easy conscience, the manifestations of a deep distress of self-esteem, suffocating feelings of inner emptiness, apathy of personal concern in most areas other than intellectual endeavor, lack of initiative, and frequently a sheer refusal to function socially. I recoiled in horror, seeing in myself the identical malady with which I had so arduously tried to enable my clients to come to terms—their narcissistic disturbance. It was not that I had been unaware of my narcissism before. But rather than regarding my narcissism as *my affliction,* I had viewed it simply as another of my personal traits, like my vertebrate stubbornness. Once I seized upon an idea or a venture, it took considerable argument or consequence to dissuade me from its pursuit. I recall that when in my early twenties while in psychotherapy with a rather well-known analyst in New

York, I had vigorously argued and tried to convince him that suffering was necessary for creative endeavor, that no truly creative person could escape emotional pain as a mainspring of his existential struggle. I am reminded now as I write of the words of the character in Pirandello's play:[1]

> For man never reasons so much and becomes so introspective as when he suffers; since he is anxious to get at the cause of his suffering, to learn who has produced them, and whether it is just or unjust that he would have to bear them. On the other hand, when he is happy, he takes his happiness as it comes and doesn't analyze it, just as if happiness were his right.... [P. 267]

My analyst remained unconvinced of my argument. I have, as a therapist myself during the years, modified my viewpoint about the neurotic elements in suffering; yet I have remained as ardent in my willingness to forge my art with the anguish of my personal struggles. I have exclaimed that

> My trek from the journey of life will always be to the outside of things—boring away at the superficial and holy with equal endeavor, taunting the established as to the right to self-respect and contentment.
> I will never be considered competent or desirable—as to equal regard with other men—I will always be "the weary, way-worn wanderer" who will perpetually seek some native shore, and will find all empty, cold, and homeless.

As the Don Juan character I depicted earlier, my creative Self has grown out of the languish and despair of my rejected Self. This is a Self which felt compelled to a destiny which the poetess Ann Sexton has presented so poignantly (see chapter five). I realize that Sexton's words, like that of my own, have been uttered out of a philosophical depression. Yet, narcissistically, I have wanted to believe these words, to justify my rebuff from others as their trepidation, the threat of my courage to face up to my own pain and that of theirs, to take the hard road in a quest for identity and substance. I rejoiced at times at others scoffing at my struggles with pain. I claimed that if they had treated me better, they would have defined my well-being and, as such, would have robbed me of defining myself. However, a certain uneasiness gnawed in me. I had to seriously question whether my philosophical depression was simply a masochistic stance, the only way I would permit myself in the dark hours of my life to create and sustain meaning for my existence.

Having questioned my philosophical depression, I had to, concomitantly, question my courage and my honesty. This was a far more anguished introspection for me than most other sorts of self-inquiry. If I found my courage and my honesty illusionary, then I would be left empty. For these attributes have been my ontological anchorages—the Self-reported reasons for enduring my ontological pain. I have always claimed that I must be more honest and more courageous than others. Like the Don Juan character, I have chosen these attributes as my uniqueness. As such I could not allow myself mitigation of the anguish I sensed in my vulnerability to a sense of denigration of my own self-esteem. But what if my purported self-honesty and courage were merely masochistic ploys to cover and protect me from more painful truths about myself! Ironically, am I honest and courageous enough to pursue this potential deception and follow it to its burning core? I was and am still not certain.

A friend and colleague jolted me with the statement that my defiance, periods of aloofness, and willingness to undergo my difficult struggles alone, were attempts to deny my very deep need to please others. Her statement had considerable impact on me. She was probably quite right! But how can I be certain? What are my credentials for assuming that I can come to terms with my own struggles? I have come to realize that my professional credentials are insufficient alone to qualify me as my own healer. For, indeed, part of the cost of gaining these credentials was the neglect of attention to my need to develop an inner core of security and self-esteem that derives from pursuing mutually gratifying and caring relationships with others. I now realize that instead of relationships, I was programmed for productivity, And, as creatively as I was allowed to express myself, still I did not have permission for enjoyment. Whatever I produced wasn't good enough or simply was not enough.[2] So I strove for greater and greater proficiency—first as an athlete in my youth when I entered college. But because whatever I did had to be the best, giving the endeavor my entire body and my soul, I could not devote sufficient energies to athletics, school work, and the other areas of my life. Because I could not sufficiently care for myself, perhaps simply because I did not know how, I invested more in my image than in trying to fill the emptiness within me. I chose to devote the energies I spent in athletics in scholarship, and after graduate school, in writing and professional skill proficiency.

The examination of my ideas and sentiments in trying to write about them and experience them in the struggles of my clients evoked considerable perturbed self-consciousness in me. The more I learned about myself and those with whom I worked, the more I was forced to ask myself, "What is it all about? What is my existence all about?" The more I learn about myself and others, the more I realize and have become concerned by the increasing awareness of all I have successfully avoided.

I found myself in a marriage in which I put the blame on my wife for what I was missing in my existence. Whatever I did wasn't good enough or proficient enough for her. I never had in her eyes the right for satisfaction, self-concern, and self-worth. I was not allowed to doubt her or myself but, instead, perpetually was caught up in a mindless, fanatical compulsion to keep doing more and more, to become more recognized and professionally respected, without ever having the right to ask "Why?" She dismissed my uniqueness and my achievements, notwithstanding. Instead, she berated me for not being involved in the mundane pursuits of her friends' husbands. I regarded them as undifferentiated stiffs—all looking, sounding, and undoubtedly smelling alike, all marching to the same monotonous, mindless drum. But I slowly but inevitably came to realize that she appeared only as I needed her to be—the unreasonable, selfish shrew, the critical, ungiving taskmaster—which my philosophical depression required. I came to realize that I doubted my own capacity to love and care for others and, for that matter, to be loved and cared for by others. As a consequence, I had found someone—regardless of how bright, talented, and attractive she was—who continually let me know that my caring wasn't good enough (or, for that matter, that my capacity for caring was nonexistent) and that I was unworthy of being cared for in return. I could with this pathos then go on in romantic despair and justified resentment for not having to care for myself or to have to reach out to others. To hide and divert the emotional impotence and pain I experienced, I kept producing as a therapist, writer, and educator. But, finally, I found that I could not continue as a therapist, because I realized that I was a hypocrite. I was not dealing with the very issues that I expected my clients to confront and work through. I could tolerate almost any other weakness in myself—but not hypocrisy. It was too allied with my need to see myself as courageous and honest. Oh, what stirring reverberations I had with the character of Dysart when I first saw *Equus* on Broadway! I experienced critical attacks on the integrity of Dysart's struggles in the play as personal attacks on my own integrity.

To escape inertia, I had to leave my marriage. To leave my marriage, I had to leave my practice. My relationship with my wife was for many years essentially a business relationship, and it was bad business for me—all cost, no profit! About two and a half years before the publication of this book I terminated my practice—six private therapy groups a week, four of which I conducted as co-therapist with my wife, and all the other direct clinical work I had been doing for many years. I moved away and have spent the last two years and a half traveling. I have taught in three or four different cities a month and have given workshops around the country and in Europe. Occasionally I do a client consultation for a colleague when visiting another city. I had for two years also retained a few, never more than five, therapy hours a week.

What more is there for me as a therapist? I question whether, indeed, I will continue as a therapist. But I cannot really answer this at this moment. What is clear, however, is that I cannot be the kind of therapist I was when I made a decision to become a therapist, nor, for that matter, the kind of therapist I have been. It is not that I regret that I became a psychologist and a therapist. Even were I to choose again, I could choose nothing so congruently with what my needs have been. Nor is it that when I practiced I wasn't a useful and effective therapist. This is simply not the issue! The question for me is, "What am I to become as a person?" Perhaps I must become a healer to myself, but I realize that this task cannot be borne alone. The journey into Self requires the presence of another. The last two years and a half has been an attempt on my part to engage my friends and those with whom I encounter along my journeys to explore myself as openly as I can. I have utilized the skills I acquired in my practice to face up to the issues and concerns I had previously avoided by becoming a practitioner. I have been particularly interested in looking at ways that bring myself and others into experiencing and utilizing parts of ourselves which we have heretofore avoided experiencing.[3]

Would I prefer to give up my narcissism? I don't know! I must pay close attention to my stubbornness and fortitude, this I am aware of; it is the best of what I am and certainly the worst of what I can be. My persistence, the tenacious hold I assert on ideas and ambitions, the pursuit of excellence and enlightened ways of being, together with my unwillingness to be stopped by pain or conflict, have carried me past the mass of wishy-washy, uncertain men. Yet whatever cost my narcissism has borne me, it considerably more frightens me to abandon myself in a world without heroism and ambition. There is something strange and malevolent about being reconciled to a world where egoism is being denigrated, where the concepts of "I" and "me" are regarded as personal obscenities.

Chapter Seven

The Paradoxical Journey
in Search of Self

"All Cretans are liars."

–Epimenides of Crete,
sixth century B.C.

Once I stood on a very high summit. Below me everything appeared quite small but perspicuously evident. I felt content in having found a unique perspective into the world below me in which I dwell. As I turned to leave I happened to glance behind me. I was startled to realize that out of my sight initially stood a much higher hill. Undoubtedly I would find a much clearer perspective on my world on the hill in back of me. I felt a sense of nausea in having been deluded by my ignorance.

The futile zeal to overcome the nausea of our ever-increasing awareness of our ignorance is demonstrated in the parable of the intrepid seeker of the meaning of life. This young man devoted his life to a quest for universal and everlasting meaning. He devoured every scholarly work he could find purporting wisdom. He visited museums and works of art. None of these contained the wisdom for which he searched. He sought out scholars in universities and scientists in their laboratories and the halls of sciences. He even tried out every known variety of psychotherapy, and this endeavor kept him occupied for many years, as there were many. He found the therapies circumscribed, the scholars and scientists finite and unconvincing. No longer a young man, the seeker was finally prepared to relent from his journey for wisdom. It was then that he heard of a man who lived in a remote village high in the Himalaya mountains. His informants told the seeker that this sage was undoubtedly the wisest man in the world. After many months of preparation and difficult journey, the seeker finally reached the summit of the mountain and the village in which the sage resided. The seeker, journey-worn as he may have been, nonetheless raced into the village calling out the name of the renowned guru. He was led to the far reaches of the village. He was directed into a tent where he encountered the most profoundly per-ceptive-appearing old man he had ever set his eyes upon. The key to the meaning of life seemed but only a moment away. He blurted out his zeal-ous inquiry, the answer to which he had sought for so long:

> "The meaning of Life," he was cheerfully and promptly told by the old sage, "is a field of wheat."

> "What?" exclaimed the seeker, not certain if the wise old man had under-stood his question. "The meaning of life is a wheat field?"

> "You mean the meaning of life is not a field of wheat?" blurted back the old man in surprise and dismay.

Modern man has become in his own presence problematic to himself. He seems further from understanding himself than when he first began to explore his own identity (Barrett, 1958). Kierkegaard analogously tells us that modern man is hardly aware that he exists, until he wakes up to find himself dead. (I discussed my own realization of this dilemma in the last chapter.) Yet, paradoxically, no age has become as self-conscious as our own. Can modern man awaken himself from the confines of his illusionary self-consciousness and find the possibility of a genuine and authentic exist-ence? To examine this question, we first must take full cognizance of the as-sumptions of thought instilled in us and encouraged by our own Western culture.

Western Thought

Western philosophy, the discipline that endeavors to convey knowl-edge about the nature of man and his world to the constituents of Western society, is based upon the venerable exercises of *logical* and *rational* con-straints to thinking. These constraints are part of a language game played by rather definitive rules. The rules informing these exercises are composed of certain suppositions that cannot be put to test. In short, logical thought is derived from reasoning that follows from its premises. Like all exercises and games, whether language-based or not, logical thought starts from given premises that cannot be questioned or doubted, for to do so an endless progression of questions would ensue which never can be finally substantiated. For example, science—the product of a logical language exercise—in choosing prediction as one of the objectives of the game it plays, must then posit that the relations between events are bound together in a causal sequence. Questions about certainty must be held in abeyance to be scientific. If the player does not accept this rule, or constraint, then he cannot play the game called "science."

Logic, then, tells us nothing about the real world. Logic only reports to us what would follow *if* a hypothetical situation, consisting of several basic assumptions, *were* true. It also is a practical language game, for the most part, enabling its participants to communicate thoughts, feelings, and intentions in a systematic and agreed-upon manner. The dissolution of any logical argument, therefore, is to simply state, "I don't accept your premises!"

The second component of Western thought is rationality. Rationality is another language game which maintains that cognitive reasoning enables the Self to best understand the world in which he exists by putting to test certain hunches about how events occur in nature. Rationality is based on the premise that the Self can predict the course of events by first observing prior events, seizing upon certain patterns and similarities contained in each of these events, in contrast to all other events, and as a result classify these purveyed events into distinct categories. This is to say, by selecting events which more or less accord identical patterns to earlier observed events, an observer can predict the course of this event. The crucial consideration in this exercise is that the observer apprehends *core* (or key) elements in what he observes and follows the activity of these elements in the development of a pattern in subsequent events. As a consequence of their performance in past events, he predicts activity of core elements in future events.

The great efficacy of rational thought relates to its focus on key elements in events, while ignorning the plethora of other elements in these events. It should be obvious that any attempt to follow and account for every element in any given event is highly inefficient and uncertain—as not all elements can be systematically patterned and, hence, are not predictable. This is to say that every event, like every snowflake, is unique. Any two events are never identical. Only by reducing events to a limited number of key elements can consistency of patterning be assured. In this regard psychiatry, as a rational discipline, as I have argued throughout this volume, is predicated upon reductionistic endeavor.

If we endeavored to dissolve the potency of rational reasoning we could do so by requiring the rational agent to predict and account for the activities of elements which were not focused upon or were discarded as nonessential in previous events.

My point in this discussion is to demonstrate that all language games, as all attempts to know the world, are highly selective and limited. So, for example, if a man simply wished to make love to a woman but didn't care how she experienced the encounter, it would be rational to find out what it took for her to physically respond to seduction. To take into consideration any other aspect of her experience is not rational, for it might get in the way of his intent. However, not to take her feelings into account divests the experience of much of its meaningfulness. But in this endeavor what is meaningful is not necessarily rational to the man's intent.

Western thought derives from the premise that man's mastery over his existence emanates from his interpreting the laws of nature. Having mastered the laws of nature, man can then control and direct nature by anticipating (predicting) the lawful actions of animate and inanimate objects. In this endeavor the rationalist is asked to assume an indifferent (an unbiased) attitude toward the outcome of his observations. There is ample reason for this requirement. Evidence throughout the annals of science (Rosenthal, 1976) has demonstrated that if an observer has a bias or is ego-invested in the outcome of his observations, his investment can and does influence, often radically, the outcome of his observations.

In contrast, Eastern thought is based upon the premise that man is nature and therefore cannot stand apart from nature in such a way as to objectively observe nature. In Eastern philosophy man is exhorted to act with, or perhaps better stated, to act *from* nature. As such, control and prediction of events are neither possible nor useful. Man comes to know the world by the unfolding of the world within himself.

It is not, of course, a question of which of these philosophies and ways of thought is valid. Who can say? How can we demonstrate their comparative validity? I am concerned with each of these ways of thought as *Weltanschauung,* intended to enable the Self to best deal with the world in which it finds himself emersed. As a social philosopher, I am not concerned with truth but with *functionality*. This is to say, what are the consequences for the Self in assuming and acting from each of these ways of thought? As a psychotherapist, I am concerned with the implications of these ways of thought on the people with whom I am in therapuetic encounter. Watts (1961) has written cogently in examining the implications of Western thought on psychiatry and psychology:

> At the present time psychology and psychiatry are in a state of great theoretical confusion. It may sound strange to say that most of this confusion is due to unconscious factors, for is it not the particular business of these sciences to understand "the unconscious"? But the unconscious factors bearing upon psychotherapy go beyond the traumas of infancy and the repressions of anger and sexuality. For example, the psychotherapist carries on his work with an almost wholly unexamined "philosophical unconscious." He tends to be ignorant, by reason of his highly specialized training, not only of the contemporary philosophy of science, but also of the hidden metaphysical premises

which underlie all the main forms of psychological theory. . . . . The difficulty is that man can hardly think or act at all without some kind of metaphysical premise, some basic axiom which he can neither verify nor fully define. Such axioms are like the rules of games: some give ground for interesting and fruitful plays and some do not, but it is always important to understand as clearly as possible what the rules are. [Pp. 26–27]

These language games and ways of thought are important to psychiatry insofar as they serve to divert us from viewing the ontological dilemmas inherent in emotional suffering. All systems of psychotherapy probably help to explain and to lucidate the conflicts of at least some of our clients. But each fails with at least some of the clients whom we refer to as "difficult." For these recalcitrants we fashion still more systems of psychotherapy and so on, *ad infinitum.*

What we need to recognize is that what we assign the "mentally ill" as possessing and acting from is inherent in being human. These feelings and moods are unavoidable characteristics of the person who is in touch with the frailties, paradoxes, and absurdities of the human situation (Goldberg, 1977[a]). Basic to our human condition is the gnawing fear of openly recognizing our tenuous being-in-the-world, that is, our uncertainty and our lack of control over our existence. The process of socialization is, in large part, intended to both help us deny, as well as to overcome our fragile presence in the world. We have been socially rewarded for ways of being that avoid thoughts and feelings that expose our ontological vulnerability. Our daily roles and relationships are generally designed to deny and buffer us from our aloneness and our existential fate—our dread of nonbeing. Our defenses against ontological dread have, as May (1977) indicates, led to alienation of modern man. May tells us:

As citizens of our age of technology, we are lived by our techniques. We become psychological robots, spending our lives going through the motions which we feel are ours but which are actually determined largely by forces of which we are unaware. This does not represent the "natural human condition," but expresses the illness of our age, indeed the disintegration of our times. . . . Mesmerized by the power of the success of our technology, we operate under a mass hypnosis which seems to take away individual responsibility and sap human freedom, leaving people with no choice and no will. . . .

In this respect, when was the last time the reader *actually experienced* his Self in the world rather than experiencing the assumptions and interpretations (bias) he has learned, in most part unwittingly, from other Selves about what it is to be human and to move about in the world? For example, what wine have we tasted whose quality and flavor hasn't already been determined by someone else's preferences? Or when was the last time we experienced our own walk—the actual physical sensation of our feet touching the ground?

Psychotherapy, in my view, should stand antithetical to these socialized "realities." Psychotherapy, in contrast to our typical everyday pursuits, by examining the assumptions and premises with which the Self maintains its existence, should enable the Self to separate from nuclear masses and become a differentiated individual. In this context, Watts (1961) has argued that the major function of psychotherapy is to dissipate illusion from the individual's perception. He writes:

> If, then, there is to be fruitful development in the science of psychotherapy, as well as in the lives of those whom it intends to help, it must be released from the unconscious blocks, unexamined assumptions, and unrealized nonsense problems which lie in its social context. [P. 29]

An Ontological Basis for Psychotherapy

Psychotherapy is akin to the process of life which is a process of separating from nuclear masses. It is this similarity with life which makes psychotherapy real. For psychotherapy to lose this unique feature is to make it artificial (Goldberg, 1977[a]). Psychotherapy, in my view, is an educative endeavor in which the client is enabled to come to a more profound appreciation of his own values by coming to terms with the assumptions by which he views the world. As I have argued in chapter four, the world in which we live—when stripped of the myriad of theory, explanation, and preconceived notions—is a big, booming, buzzing confusion. There is no direct correlation between the objective dimensions of the world and what registers on our sense receptors. In order to engage and come to terms with the complexity of our world—or even to survive within the confusion that engulfs our thoughts and feelings—we must make some semblance of meaning of our sensory and kinesthetic experiences. Although we have no assurance that our interpretation of experience is correct, we are continually compelled to make inferences (assumptions) about what is going on in the world around us. We generally respond to the universe in a dual manner. We behave in a way that is intended to achieve a preferred state of affairs, while at the same time we act in such a way as to confirm our assumptions about what we have predicted would happen as a result of our actions. Often we achieve confirmation of our assumptions at the expense of our personal freedom. When we avoid situations that are complex, ambiguous, or require weighing of possibilities, our expectations about ourselves are confirmed. We acquire a sense of certainty because the confirmation allows us to believe, however mistakenly, that we are being taken care of in the precarious world we inhabit (Goldberg, 1977[a]). The realization of personal responsibility is predicated upon the Self's commitment to withstand varying degrees of discomfort and risk in questioning the validity of certain of its assumptions about the external world (Goldberg, 1973). In this regard it is necessary that both therapist and client explore the implicit assumptions from which they experience and enact their relationship, questioning what they do as a result of their assumptions about the other (Goldberg, 1977[a]). In short, in order to come to terms with the conflictive presses of contemporary society, the client needs not just another technique or another therapeutic experience. He requires another "strategy" involving a different perspective from which to view the conflictive assumptions and dilemmas he has accrued in his being-in-the-world.

Paradoxical Approaches to Psychotherapy

Sylvester has written:

> As lightning clears the air of inpalpable vapours, so incisive paradox frees human intelligence from the lethargic influence of latent and unsuspected assumptions. Paradox is the slayer of prejudice [1978].

The difference between paradoxical approaches, at least as I employ them, and other therapeutic systems is that the latter are generally based upon what "is," while the former are experiential-inventive—questioning assumptions about what is commonly regarded as "reality." Paradoxical approaches are less concerned with "truth" or "fact" as they are with Nietzsche's caution, "Can it be lived (by the client)?" I assume that truth is paradoxical. Each article of wisdom contains within its own contradiction. This means to me that *truths stand side by side.* In Western thought, logical sequences rule our reason, and by so doing, dominate our psychology. We need to realize that our attitudes, feelings, and behaviors rest upon assumptions—which we rarely question. The core assumption in many cases is of a logical, sequential universe in which if A is true and B is logically converse, then B cannot be valid. In the paradoxical mode each may be simultaneously meaningful. Contradictory truths do not necessarily cancel each other out or dominate each other, but stand side by side, inviting participation and experimentation. Rather than to give weight to factual or logical discourse, the paradoxical practitioner frequently may state his disagreement simultaneously with his agreement by saying to each "And this is also true!" As the client leans in any one direction, the practitioner may nudge him in another. For example, to those clients who express their appreciation for the therapist's help, he may question the power they permit him to influence them. To those who complain that he isn't helping them, he may suggest that they stand on their heads to keep from rolling over.

Paradoxical approaches are employed to enable clients to participate actively in situations they have heretofore felt compelled to avoid. The British clinical psychologist Donald Bannister (1978), although speaking in more essentialistic terms than I would ascribe to, gives us some lucidity into the concerns I am addressing when he indicates that for many of the clients he works with what has gone awry

> is a misformulation of the problem. That is, I don't ignore what he says is wrong but I want the right to question it, and question it repeatedly, because the reason he never solved it was perhaps that it wasn't the problem.

Paradoxical psychotherapy is not inconsistent with psychodynamic therapy. However, it is frequently a more direct intervention, in the sense of getting the client to experientially realize that his fears need to be re-experienced and completed so that they lose their residual tension. If a fear prevents a client from experiencing a condition or a situation, the anxiety and tension built up in regard to these conditions cannot be discharged. The experience of not being able to discharge the aversive affect reciprocally "justifies" the avoidance of situations that evoke similar tensions and anxieties in an ever-proliferating, stimulus-generalizing way. Specific paradoxical interventions by the therapist are often required to give the client the opportunity to experience his resistance directly or himself in another way than he typically experiences himself.

The Use of Paradox to Change Limitation to Advantage

To view the world and its human constituents paradoxically has the propensity to increase the agent's functional options. The world is manifold with possibility but, as I argued in chapter five, only to the extent that the Self conceptualizes and turns toward these possibilities. Physically, human constituents are limited in their access to the resources of the world in which they dwell. There are only so many jobs, desirable other Selves for involvement, and so forth. The use of paradoxical exploration in many instances may unfold each limitation on physical resource as a psychological possibility (advantage).

The case of Barney Norton[1] demonstrates this contention. Barney, a bright and conscientious recent college graduate, had considerable difficulty securing a job in his major field in college, communications, because of the large abundance of job applicants for a limited number of available positions. I indicated to Barney that this limitation actually created the possibility of a position which might not have been as available if an abundance of positions were present. Indeed, Selves, in their *sansara* or social myopia, often miss possibility to the extent that they accord with Western logic, which often is to pursue the obscure and disregard the obvious. It should be obvious that if there are not enough positions, then there is a need for a person to create more jobs or at least to enable job applicants to improve their skills so as to more favorably compete for available positions. An obscure attitude is to wait around for someone else to provide a position for Barney. The obvious strategy, then, is the use of creative Self in contrast to the reactive Self illustrated by the obscure attitude. Barney was told by this author to create for himself a position as a consultant and employment counselor who seeks positions in the communications field for other job applicants. By employing his own experience and difficulty in trying to secure jobs, Barney could use this information to organize a service in which experts in the field could provide information and training to help applicants improve their job skills and ability to secure positions.

In the next chapter I will describe in considerable detail several clinical situations in which paradoxical approaches were utilized by this author.

Chapter Eight

Paradoxical Approaches
in Psychotherapy

"It isn't that my theory is wrong; it is that the facts are misleading."
—actor Paul Lukas in the movie
"The Lady has Vanished"

There is a tale told from ancient time about a lovely maiden whose greatest joy came from gazing upon herself in the reflection of her morning bath. One dark morning she looked into her bath and found with horror that the figure she saw reflected had no head. She became hysterical and rushed around, shrieking, "My head is gone! Where is my head? Who has my head? I shall surely perish if I don't find it!"

Even though her friends tried to assure her that she still had her head on, she refused to believe them. She insisted that every time she looked at her reflection, her head was missing.

Suddenly one day one of her friends gave her a sharp clout on her head. She cried out in pain and her friend exclaimed, "That is your head. There it is. It was there all the time." The maiden began to realize that she had somehow deluded herself into thinking that she had no head, when in fact she always had a head.

So it is with our ability to make sense of our existence. We are not always able to do so, because the perspective we assume is too limited, or because we lack the momentary clarity to recognize what is already there.

The art of psychotherapy is characterized by the endeavor not to be averted by the recalcitrance of the practitioner's clients. In this pursuit practitioners have continually sought newer and more impactful therapeutic approaches. In recent years there has been considerable interest in a closely related assortment of therapeutic techniques predicated on the recognition that the practice of psychotherapy is in many ways inherently paradoxical. These special maneuvers and interventions seem ostensibly designed to thwart the goals of therapy, but are actually formulated to achieve these goals (Rohrbaugh, et al., 1977). Referred to as "therapeutic paradox," "paradoxical intention," "paradigmatic strategy," "going with the resistance," "siding with the resistance," "joining the resistance," "mirroring," "provocative therapy," "absurd psychotherapy," "acting in intervention," "negative practice," "symptom scheduling," "implosion," "flooding," and "reverse psychology," among various appellations, these techniques have been described in the literature by practitioners of such diverse therapeutic orientations as Dunlap (1928), Rosen (1953), Lindner (1955), Wolpe (1958), Frankl (1960), Haley (1963), Kopp (1972), Spotnitz (1976), Stampfl (1977), and Whitaker (1978). Paradoxical interventions have been found by these practitioners useful in a wide variety of treatment and pedagogic situations in which more common and straightforward approaches prove to be minimally effective, and in many instances, antagonistic to therapeutic progress.

I will in this chapter describe a number of clinical and pedagogic situations in which I have employed paradoxical approaches to enable the people with whom I have worked to regain the clarity to see what is already there, by questioning the assumptions upon which their myopia emanates.

Most people enter psychotherapy, because they are overwhelmed with how they should be constituted and feel they cannot actualize, or because they are concerned because they "feel nothing." In either of these cases, they are generally dissatisfied with the direction that their existence has taken them. In still other instances, people feel "forced" to enter psychotherapy by the persuasion or coercion of others, and these clients, understandably to various degrees and in a multifold of different ways, resist treatment. I have found that the contractual approach, which I have described in some detail in a previous book (see Goldberg, 1977a), and which I have aimed for in my practice, does not have to be abandoned with resistant clients. I realize that all clients that I work with are, in varying degrees, characterologically unwilling or unable to assume a responsible relationship with me. If they could, they probably wouldn't be seeking psychological amelioration. To varying degrees, clients generally prefer to assume positions of confusion, helplessness, and inadequacy, or indifference—in order to be saved by the omniscient magic of the therapist or to have fulfilled their belief that their personal situation is without remedy, so that they can legitimately continue to harbor resentment and hurt and react with retaliatory mechanisms toward themselves and/or others. I try, therefore, to work from whatever attitude the client comes with, to engage him in a relationship in which I provide him with the opportunity to negotiate for becoming the kind of person he wishes to be. I will illustrate my strategy with an example of my work with a most recalcitrant client.

Mr. Jones had reluctantly consulted me as a private practitioner on the advice of his attorney. He had been charged on two occasions with sexually molesting small children. He would shortly be brought to court on criminal charges. His attorney advised him that the court would probably look more favorably upon him if he voluntarily sought psychiatric help and entered into a treatment program. His attorney also advised him to consult a psychologist or psychiatrist, because a doctor held more weight with the court than did other mental health workers. Mr. Jones, a poorly articulate and ill-educated person, was a passive-dependent person of around fifty years of age who had a chronic alcoholic pattern. Both incidents supposedly occurred while he was intoxicated. He saw no need for psychological treatment. He claimed that he recently began seeing an alcoholism counselor who had helped him stop drinking (as a "result" of two sessions). Since both incidents occurred while he was intoxicated, he claimed his desisting from further imbibing would guarantee that these incidents would never again occur. But, Mr. Jones added, he would go along with my recommendations.

A few months after I began seeing Mr. Jones, he was given a five-year suspended sentence by the court. His probation was based upon the provision that he be "under a doctor's care" for the period of probation. The terms of the "doctor's care" were left vague and ambiguous. I did not feel entirely comfortable with continuing to work with Mr. Jones once he had received a sentence. I had no doubts that he would have discontinued psychotherapy had his probation not required it. Consequently, he had not freely contracted to work with me. Upon thinking about this, however, it occurred to me that this was overly idealistic and inane reasoning. Freedom and choice cannot realistically be conceptualized as absolutes; they are only possible with a defined situation. Although there were serious consequences for our actions, Mr. Jones and I still had the freedom to discontinue working with each other. Mr. Jones did not have to accept me as a therapist; the area in which I practice is saturated with psychotherapists. I chose to work with Mr. Jones because he was paying me a reasonable fee and because I felt that I might be of help to him. Despite his inarticulateness and stubbornness, I found him likable. Although I could have chosen to delimit Mr. Jones's freedom if I acted as a representative of the legal system that had the delegated power to control his behavior, I chose instead to be in no way responsible to report Mr. Jones's behavior inside or outside therapy to anyone. Nevertheless, because his freedom from a prison sentence was dependent upon his attendance in psychotherapy, I agreed to report his attendance at sessions to his probation officer, but only if this information was requested of me (it never was requested).

Given psychotherapy as an alternative to prison, Mr. Jones had more of a choice in how he would use the sessions than in whether he would attend them. Since he was paying for the sessions, it was his prerogative to use them as he wished. It was my responsibility to explore with him in language he could relate to my notions about what psychotherapy was about and what it could and could not reasonably accomplish for him. Mr. Jones had grown up in a rural mountain area. I made frequent analogies to raising crops and animals and educating young children for responsibility to relate my notions about psychotherapeutic work to experiences with which Mr. Jones could identify. I made specific recommendations about how he might use the sessions in terms of the difficulites he was experiencing in his marriage.

Mr. Jones expressed more annoyance than guilt about the events that had caused him legal difficulty. He blamed them on the abuse he received from his wife and his stepchildren. With minimal insight and even less guilt about his behavior, a scrutiny of Mr. Jones's developmental history could well have taken up the five years of probation without necessarily modifying his character structure or leading to mastery over his marital situation, so I suggested that the focus during the sessions be contemporary. Because he was a very withdrawn person whose only significant, albeit conflictive relationships were with his wife and his stepchildren, I recommended that his family join him in his sessions. He readily agreed, because he maintained that it was his wife's neglect of him that forced him to commit the acts that required him to see me for psychotherapy.

He spent most of the sessions complaining about his wife's mistreatment of him. In reaction, Mrs. Jones expressed frustration and resentment that he was not willing to articulate or demonstrate any caring for her. Ironically, despite the legal and moral difficulties he found himself in, Mr. Jones was a person with a strong sense of justice. Indeed, his morality conflicted with his wife's childish, impulsive, and irresponsible system for relating with others. It was at those times when his wife treated him unfairly, depriving him of sexual and affectionate caring, that he became intoxicated. Mr. Jones, in turn, used his lack of emotional expression to punish his wife. He refused to express caring for her because he claimed, "It ain't do any good!" She retaliated by impulsively spending money on commodities he regarded as "junk." Mr. Jones became more resentful and withdrawn. Mrs. Jones, in reaction, refused to attend any more therapy sessions. Their respective systems of equity came into volatile conflict in her justifying her withdrawal from therapy by saying, "The court told you that you have to go to treatment. I don't have to go to the doctor. Only you do!"

Their marital relationship was based on a revenge contract. They were implicitly saying to each other:

MRS. JONES   If you don't express caring for me, then I won't give you any emotional support. I will not only withold sexual relations, I will also make you suffer your psychotherapy treatment as punishment rather than attend sessions so that we can work as partners in a relationship.

MR. JONES   If you don't treat me fairly, I'll withdraw from you, get drunk, and withold money from you, since that is all you seem to want from me.

The revenge contract in their relationship resulted in a "Mexican standoff." As each basically mistrusted other people, neither would retract sufficiently his or her wont to hurt so that the other could take a psychological risk and express caring. Neither of the Joneses had had sufficient experience in a trusting relationship in their personal development. Each required immediate payment in order to give to another person.

To resolve this difficult impasse, several contractual issues had to be dealt with. For Mr. Jones, money had a punitive value within the therapeutic situation. He was paying me for treatment which in his perception was punishment for having committed a socially unacceptable act. On casual observation the reader may regard Mr. Jones's situation as atypical – a resistive client forced to pay for treatment he prefers not to receive. If the reader looks more closely at the function of money in psychotherapy, he soon realizes that money is frequently an inintended but quite real punishment, even for clients who willingly and enthusiastically pursue treatment. In short, meaningful and productive psychotherapy is less expensive than incompetent and unproductive work. In productive contractual psychotherapy, client and practitioner arrive together at goals and pursue them in a mutually agreed upon fashion. Their work is efficient because they have agreed on what they are seeking and how to evaluate what they achieve together. In unproductive and uncontractual therapy, the therapist is rewarded for his inefficiency until such time as the client finally has enough sense to terminate the relationship. [I have been told that there is or was a therapist in New York City whose "therapeutic technique" consisted of saying, "put the $40 down on the table and leave."]

Mr. Jones had less freedom to terminate therapy than do other clients who are not having their attendance monitored by a governmental agency. If he dropped out of treatment, his behavior would more likely be regarded as his unwillingness to be helped, rather than as a result of my incompetence. Moreover, because Mr. Jones appeared to trust me more than he did most other people, he was unlikely to seek another practitioner regardless of how ineffectual I might be in handling his situation. Thus, I could continue to see him and have him pay me every week regardless of his progress. Indeed, I could reap more financial rewards for his lack of progress than from having him improve sufficiently that the requirement of psychotherapy might be removed from his probation. Consequently, to restore power to Mr. Jones, I had to transform money from a vehicle of punishment to a source of reward. To do this I had to act against my own financial interest. Mr. Jones regarded his psychologicl treatment as a five-year sentence, regardless of his progress; therefore, he had little incentive to take his efforts in therapy seriously. If, however, he could pay increasingly less money for therapy based on his taking psychological risks, he would then have a clear and meaningful incentive for taking therapy seriously.

I also felt that it was crucial to bring Mrs. Jones back into the sessions. She would not return unless he articulated caring for her, so I said to Mr. Jones in a session, "It seems to me that you care for your wife, but that you refuse to give her the satisfaction of letting her know that you do." He replied that while this might be true, he would not tell her that he cared because it wouldn't do him any good. She would continue to treat him unfairly.

I offered Mr. Jones what I referred to as a "no-financial-risk gamble." I told him, "You say that if you told your wife that you cared for her, she would ignore your statement and just treat you as badly as before you made the statement. What if you could gamble on your point of view and if you were wrong you would win some money? I say this because you have expressed to me the concern that coming to these sessions week after week is expensive. Therefore, I will charge you one dollar less on your next session, provided you tell your wife that after a discussion with me you realized that you cared for her, and, provided she responds favorably to your statement, contrary to how you believe she will respond. On the other hand, if she responds as you claim she will, the bill will stay the same for the next session, but you will have lost nothing."

Participants in a family therapy group are members of a natural group who have the ability to reward and punish one another in continuing and binding ways. By "disinheriting" family members they deprive them of the ability to viably negotiate for their needs and desires within the family. The reader may be aware that I was employing a combination of behaviorial and paradoxical models in my attempt to restore power to Mr. Jones by providing him with an opportunity for negotiating for more favorable conditions within our therapeutic relationship. Parenthetically, I am generally opposed to using behavioral approaches that "solve" patient "problems." However, when the existential concerns in the relationship are elucidated, behavioral techniques are frequently efficacious in reciprocal exchanges between the therapeutic agents. Moreover, I have found paradoxical techniques to be rather useful in circumventing resistive characterological patterns. I utilize paradoxical techniques (Frankl, 1969) to enable clients to participate actively in situations they have heretofore felt compelled to avoid.

These techniques have an absurd aspect. Mr. Jones would reap a financial reward by demonstrating that his limited but entrenched view of his wife was invalid. In the past, his anger and withdrawal evoked a predictably unfavorable response from her. As a person with a strongly moralistic orientation, Mr. Jones was rewarded with moral indignation. The situation that I presented him with, on the other hand, provided him with an incentive for proving himself "wrong" for his lack of demonstrative caring. If Mr. Jones deviated from his characteristic withdrawal and his wife reciprocated with affection, *uncertainty* would be evoked in their normative system. If this uncertainty persisted for any period of time, each would be compelled to reexamine expectations of and from each other. This reexamination would be a reconsideration of the dysfunctional contractual relationship they were currently maintaining.

I was aware, nonetheless, that there were strong forces in their relationship for avoiding this reexamination. Mr. Jones's continuing willingness to take psychological risks could not be maintained only by my rewarding him. Mrs. Jones was simply too much more a significant person for him than I was. Her power to punish him was considerably greater than my capacity to reward him. The principles of equity and balance (Goldberg, 1977a) required that Mrs. Jones reward him by returning to the sessions. This was easier said than done.

Mrs. Jones was caught up in a pre-oedipal struggle between her unregulated, impulsive demands and cruel, introjected authority figures. She experienced most demands upon her as unfair. She attempted to free herself of these demands by dysfunctionally childish mechanisms, saying in effect, "If my husband expects me to be at the sessions, then I won't attend even though I actually enjoy them!" Mrs. Jones avoided facing her internal conflicts and contradictions by externalizing them. She skillfully, but unwittingly, "encouraged" her husband's angry reactions. His reactions "justified" Mrs. Jones not meeting her promises to him to attend sessions or to meet his emotional needs. As long as I or any other authority surrogate insisted that she attend sessions, she would rebel. She would only be able to get in touch with her internal contradictions at such time as she was confronted by the realization that rebellion against external objects did not rid her of her internal turmoil. Consequently, in a session that Mr. Jones attended alone, I told him that I would like him to tell his wife that she didn't have to attend sessions, and she would understand why I said this. As soon as Mr. Jones gave my message to his wife, she was on the phone yelling at me, "I know I don't have to attend sessions. You don't have to tell me that!" I pointed out that that was why I had said to her husband that she would understand. I had, with my provocative statement, made explicit the conflictive, contractual relationship between Mrs. Jones and me. I had indicated that she didn't need to rebel against her husband and me to prove that she was a voluntary participant and an adult. I went on to indicate the time of Mr. Jones's next session, adding that if she cared to, we would be glad to have her attend. She attended!

In working with the Joneses and with other clients who have considerable difficulty attempting new behavioral patterns and taking psychological risks, I have developed the following working model based upon the principles of equity and balance (Goldberg, 1977a):

1. A client will tend to experience as unfair any therapeutic task that requires him to significantly exceed previous performance.

2. The client's self-esteem tends to be increased when he is expected to perform at a level that exceeds his previous performance.

3. The more concordant his expected behavior is with known standards of conduct, the more equitable and comfortable he experiences the task.

4. The more the client feels involved in setting standards for his own behavior or is aware of the consequences of his intended future behaviors, the more equitable and comfortable he experiences his behavior as being.

5. These hypotheses taken together suggest that clients who are being asked to modify or replace value systems in seeking new behavioral modes feel uncertain as to how their intended behaviors will be judged and accepted. This suggests that a basic therapeutic task for client and therapist is to consciously evolve a normative belief system appropriate and favorable to the qualities and ways of being the client intends.

The Use of Countertransference in Paradoxical Approaches

I have been disappointed that with some of the brighter neurotics with whom I have worked, who are rather accomplished in defeating therapists; with some of the seemingly "more brilliant" paradoxical contracts I have offered them and which they initially have agreed to try, they subsequently declined becoming involved in. But I have begun to realize that these paradoxical contracts, although not enacted, nevertheless serve a therapeutic purpose. They avail themselves in a similar role to therapist interpretations in psychodynamic therapy. By having his dilemma presented in a paradoxical way, the client is afforded a new and more flexible view of his condition. Interpretations can be denied because of the client's need to rebel against the authority of the therapist. In resisting interpretative statements by the therapist, all the client is left with is a denied statement. But with paradoxical contracts, having rejected the activity suggested by the therapist to deal with his "problem," the client need not resist the meaningfulness of the statement about his limited perspective contained within that contract, and he may internalize its import.

I have also come to recognize that the arousal of certain counter-transferential elements is often indispensable in efficacious paradoxical approaches. I have found it useful at times in psychotherapy to make the assumption, as an "as if," that similar to the conservation of energy in physical systems, pathology within a social system is neither created nor destroyed. Therefore, for a client in a therapeutic system to experience himself as less pathological, the therapist may have to take on some of the client's "craziness," in that according to our assumption about pathological action, it cannot be relinquished, only transformed or transferred. Carl Whitaker's work (1978) suggests a similar approach in working with family systems.

Let me give you some examples of what I am referring to. Over ten years ago in my capacity as chief psychologist of an in-patient service at a large psychiatric hospital, I organized an out-patient clinic for patients who had been discharged. I had at the time a theoretical commitment to providing family-oriented therapy for these patients. The symptoms these patients manifested were clearly reactions to disturbed and pathological family systems. Unfortunately, I had no training in family therapy at the time. Attached to the out-patient clinic was a very energetic and pleasant young psychiatric nurse, who also had no experience in family therapy. We decided, perhaps in mutual support, to work together as co-therapists with these family systems. One of the first families we worked with was that of a woman in her mid-thirties, who recently had been discharged from the in-patient service. She had had several previous hospitalizations. She, her two small sons, and her mother joined her in family sessions. Her Greek-born mother was a strong, controlling, moralistic but rather warm and friendly woman. She looked down at her daughter as incapable of taking proper care of her children, unable to hold her husband (who had deserted the family) and as a disgrace because she would not stop acting sorry for herself. The grandmother regarded her daughter much as she did her grandchildren. It became evident to my co-therapist and I that the grandmother's tyrannical control over the life of her daughter was preventing her daughter from psychologically separating and individuating herself as a responsible adult. I sought to devise a way to loosen her grip on the family. As the reader might suspect, the grandmother was a constant worrier. During one of the sessions the grandmother reported that her own mother, well over ninety years of age, was quite ill in Greece. The grandmother indicated with considerable sadness that she might never see her mother again. We inquired why this was, why she couldn't visit her own aged and infirmed mother. The grandmother told us that she was too much needed in Washington to leave for Greece, even if this meant she would not be able to see her mother again.

She told us that it was her moral responsibility to stay in Washington and to take care of her family. Not only must her grandchildren be supervised and protected from her inadequate daughter, but her favorite child, an unmarried son, had no friends and needed someone to be there for companionship. Moreover, her younger brother, a local businessman, was experiencing financial difficulties, and she indicated to us that he required her guidance and support. As such, the event of her concern about her aged mother afforded us a propitious opportunity to deal with her control over her family.

Despite the grandmother's suffocating controls over the family, I found myself liking her. Her warmth, concern, and rather good mind, despite a lack of formal education, reminded me fondly of my own maternal grandmother. I had, part out of interest and in order to develop a relationship with the power in the family system, asked her for recipes for Greek dishes I knew my wife would like to prepare. She readily offered them to me. It seemed that she liked both my co-therapist and I, but could never quite comprehend what this psychiatry talking nonsense would really accomplish. We decided to utilize the "nonsense" of psychiatry to effect a disequilibrium in the pathological family system. I indicated to the grandmother that I realized that she was an experienced and an accomplished worrier. I pointed out that she was a person who liked to worry, who did worry excessively, who generally went out of her way to worry, spent a considerable amount of time worrying, and did not share her worrying with her family. I told her that because of this I was, myself, worried about her. I was concerned that she might be getting senile. It occurred to me that she was losing a golden opportunity to really have an occasion to worry. She would probably never have a better time to worry than she had now. If she stayed in Washington she could take proper care of her family and, because her mother was old she would probably forget she had a daughter or, at least, not have enough presence of mind to resent her for not visiting her for the last time. *But* if she left for Greece she had an opportunity to worry about her lonely son for whom no one was good enough, her not-too-bright brother, her irresponsible daughter, who might take up with any man off the street, and her innocent, unprotected grandchildren. Besides, I said, as a planned afterthought, she, herself, had indicated that families were supposed to share things—good and bad—but she was too selfish to allow her family to share her worrying. She kept it all to herself, not allowing her family any morsel of her worrying. While she stayed in Washington she did all the worrying for them. They did not have to worry about each other or themselves.[1] I encouraged her to indulge herself in shared worrying as the best thing for everyone concerned. By going to Greece she could both indulge her worrying needs and give her family the opportunity to share, like all loving families should. She looked at me as if she was beginning to wonder if I might be madder than even her daughter. Her stance certainly seemed to convey that although her daughter was coming to see the "psychiatry" doctor, maybe she was all right.[2] But she did, in fact, leave for Greece a few days later. During the period of time the mother was absent from Washington and from the sessions, the daughter began to converse and respond as an adult.

The interventions utilized in the above-discussed case were based on my belief that contemporary psychotherapy frequently fails because it is based on proper procedures, which mean, in a word, to act appropriately with people who are inappropriate. Indeed, frequently the therapist needs to be appropriately inappropriate so that the clients may be less inappropriately appropriate. How appropriate is it to teach inappropriate patients how to adapt to their dehumanizing world! As a consultant to the backwards of a large psychiatric hospital, I was amazed to see the young social workers and nurses trying to teach old men, some who had been hospitalized with little or no contact with the outside world from thirty to fifty years, to try to act appropriately in their alien world. Of course, it never worked, to everyone's puzzlement and disconcertation. I suggested that in the inappropriate world in which these men lived, it was more respectful to their human dignity not to be repeatedly trying to change their inappropriate behavior but to explicitly recognize these behaviors and acknowledge the staff's concern that they were not effectively communicating with one another. Thus, for a man who had been hospitalized for thirty years, who walked through the ward loudly hallucinating, the sounds resounding like that of a roaring lion, I suggested that they give this man a megaphone to indicate that although he was trying to communicate with others and that his communications were sufficiently loud, they weren't being heard and that the staff cared and was trying to do something to bridge this gap.

In this perspective I have said to both colleagues and clients who question my paradoxical statements and ways of being: "You question whether I am straight or not, whether I mean what I am saying. You prefer to believe that the world is straight—some fixed reality and that I am being contradictory. Is it not possible that the world is paradoxical and that I am straight—relating to the world as it is!"

The use of paradoxical approaches often may enable clients to do what they *choose* to do, because they have *permission not to have* to do what they experience as their not being able to help doing. A client I had been working with in private practice for some time feared that her frequent bursts of "bitchiness" would put off and chase away the first meaningful relationship she had after many years of being a "swinger" and the girlfriend of married men. She was a woman who had considerable difficulty both expressing and being confronted with anger. I indicated that it appeared that she could not help her bitchy outbursts. The best she could do at this time was to better plan and regulate the time, place, and duration of these attacks. She was a very competent program analyst and an excellent planner. I told her to pick one day of the week when her bitchiness would be least troublesome and to use that as what I designated as a "Bitchy Day." I further suggested that she tell her fiancé about this, and if he objected to her being bitchy on that day—she was told that she was not allowed to be bitchy on any day but the designated one—that she could blame her bitchiness on me. In this way she could be bitchy and not have to be responsible for doing something she claimed she really did not want to do. She followed my instructions. She found it useful and gratifying to tell, first, her fiancé and after a while, others directly what she was experiencing toward them. In due time her communications were no longer bitchy but direct, and she no longer required a designated day for direct expression.

In planning my intervention I shared with my client the rationale for the suggestion. The rationale is based upon what I called "balance theory." In my first course in college in psychology I read of a study by Davis (1947) in which she found that infants, if given the opportunity for a balanced, nutritious diet would appropriately select one. Over time, however, the infant models his parents' appetites and increasingly is inclined toward imbalanced diets, preferring some foods and refusing others. In analogous fashion, I assume that each of us has a need for both pleasant and aversive experiences. People who intentionally seek out pleasant experiences will find that their bodies will push them toward aversive experiences, for example, a need to express certain feelings and intentions. However, if a person seeks out aversive experiences, intentionally, then their bodies will seek to balance the composite experience with positive activity.

Another instance of the use of absurdity to transform psychopathy will be illustrated in an account of my supervision several years ago of a clinical psychology intern who was working with an extremely disturbed patient in a large psychiatric hospital. The patient, whom I will refer to as "Mr. Webster," was a thin, black man from a rural North Carolina community, in his mid-thirties at the time I am discussing. He was referred for therapy due to his extreme isolation and autistic withdrawal from other patients. He had been unresponsive to the attention directed from ward personnel. The intern I was supervising was also from North Carolina. He was a friendly, warm, and very conscientious person concerned about ethical standards and was empirically oriented, having had considerable training in behavioral techniques.

When the young intern first met Mr. Webster, he described him as confused and disheveled in appearance and unable to give much of his personal history. His explanation for being in the hospital was that the judge sent him there because of his "insanity." After a few initial interviews and a battery of psychological tests, the intern reported that he had the very strong impression that Mr. [Webster] is retarded and possibly even organic. His speech is slow, often repetitive, and he doesn't have much insight into why he is here [at the hospital]. He did say he would like to have someone to talk to but he didn't give any reasons why. Throughout the session [reporting one particular session] there were long silences and Mr. [Webster] left the room several times to get water or a cigarette.... He said that his main problem was that he swallowed too much saliva and would have to make it go away.

The therapist had considerable difficulty moving the therapeutic dialogue onto any other level than that of the patient attending sessions because of his saliva problem. But even this concern could not be consistently engaged in, as the patient continued his long silences and frequently left the room to smoke. At other times, five or ten minutes into a session, he claimed that his mouth was dry and he could not swallow his saliva. He would then bolt up and leave the room to go down the hall to the water fountain. The therapist, conscientiously and passively, sat in his chair waiting for the patient to return. In supervision, I questioned the reasonableness of the therapist's conscientiousness and wondered whether his being more concerned about the patient's therapeutic progress was actually useful for the patient. Paradoxically, I realized that the therapist's deadly seriousness about the session mitigated against the patient actually experiencing either the consequences or the reasonableness of his own dilemma. I believed that only to the extent that the therapist could let go of his seriousness and play with the patient's absurd resistive ploys could the patient get in touch with the meaning of his personal dilemma. I suggested that when the patient started to leave the room to get water, that the therapist might race him down the hall and get to the fountain first, so that the patient would have to wait for him rather than vice versa. I alternately suggested that he leave the room before the patient returned or that he indicate to Mr. Webster that he appreciated his consideration of the therapist's valuable time schedule. The therapist might in the latter option indicate that if Mr. Webster left after five or ten minutes of a session he was obviously conveying to the therapist that he didn't need any more time than that—that the sessions were longer than he required. The therapist might then renegotiate with the patient for a short session from that session on. This renegotiation would continue each time Mr. Webster left before the session was over.

After considerable resistance to what he regarded as an interesting but not very responsible set of suggestions by me, the therapist adopted the last stance I had offered. Mr. Webster's trips down the hall were abruptly terminated after only one confrontation by the therapist. The utilization of other paradoxical interventions impeded various other resistive ploys by the patient. In fact, after some months the therapist and Mr. Webster were speaking together in earnest. Mr. Webster disclosed painful and disturbing experiences and memories about growing up on a dirt-poor chicken farm, living with a rather disturbed mother.

Interestingly, Mr. Webster no longer appeared retarded to the therapist but as an uneducated person who was in the bright-normal intelligence range and had marked schizoid features. The constituents had reached what I regarded as a rather propitious moment in their therapeutic encounter. Unfortunately, in a few months the intern would be finishing his internship and leaving the hospital. In fact, it was necessary that he return to North Carolina several times in the next few months to complete doctoral requirements and take his exams.

I believed that Mr. Webster's presenting complaint of not being able to swallow water (which had persisted despite his improved psychological functioning but was not spontaneously brought up by him anymore) was experienced by the patient as a life-and-death obsession. As he held on to his view of the world as a depriving, unpalpable world in which to exist, so he was forced to taste his unpleasant saliva without being able to swallow and extricate his biological byproduct. I believed that unless Mr. Webster could realize this in a way that made some deep impact on him—that is, only to the extent that he was willing to risk his life to transcend his psychotic view of the world—he would remain rather detached and immobilized, forever an institutionalized, custodial patient. I suggested that the therapist present this option to Mr. Webster. The intern was startled and taken aback by my suggestion. He insisted that he would have no part in an endeavor that risked Mr. Webster's life. The risk I was referring to was, of course, psychological—a commitment to a more optimistic existence rather than an issue of his physical well-being. I suggested that the therapist, as a well-read purveyor of the psychological literature, actually deal with the symptomatic problem that Mr. Webster was asking for help with, rather than regard the complaint as simply resistance, as he had up until then. The therapist might report to Mr. Webster that he had become aware of a study that suggested a means of getting rid of his saliva problem. He would need to caution Mr. Webster that the solution was a serious and risky venture—that Mr. Webster would have to risk his life to overcome the problem. Mr. Webster eagerly agreed to take this risk. He said he was willing to do anything to overcome his problem and that he trusted the therapist. The therapist said that the patient needed to hold his breath for a full minute. After a minute of doing so, Mr. Webster's problem would either be resolved or forever be irrevocable.

With considerable concern the patient wanted to know how he could ascertain that he made it through this ordeal. The therapist indicated that this, of course, was an easy matter. All he had to do was to feel his wrist and upon sensing a pulse he could be assured that his saliva problem was probably over. The patient took a deep breath. A minute or so later he looked at the therapist with askance. The therapist nodded his head and indicated that Mr. Webster should check his wrist. He did. Mr. Webster exclaimed with excitement and apparent pride that he could feel his pulse. "I can feel my pulse! I can feel my pulse! I am over the problem," he cried, running out of the room and over to every patient and staff person he found on the ward, repeating over and over his joy. The reader will remember that Mr. Webster was an almost completely withdrawn person several months prior.

I emphasized in subsequent supervision sessions that for this therapeutic strategy to become meaningful rather than simply a technique or a "trick," that the therapist must convey to Mr. Webster, to the extent he experienced, the admiration and appreciation he had for Mr. Webster's willing to risk his life to overcome his difficulties. Therapy continued without need for further techniques or ploys, with a very warm and free exchange between therapist and patient. The therapist described Mr. Webster as looking, sounding, and behaving almost unrecognizable from the man who had appeared before him six months prior.

Unfortunately, as so frequently happens in institutions with training programs, the therapist had to make a number of visits back to his university. Mr. Webster apparently experienced the therapist as having let him down. In the last month of therapy, there was considerable regression on Mr. Webster's part and insufficient time to deal with these feelings. This is a typical component of institutional psychiatry!

Group psychotherapy training and practice have been one of my major interests in psychotherapy for many years. Much of the work, theory, and practice with paradoxical approaches have emanated from my group practice. The remainder of this chapter is devoted to a discussion of paradoxical approaches in groups.

Adjunctive Paradoxical Interventions in Group Psychotherapy

To illustrate the concept of paradoxical intervention I will describe the use of this approach as a means of dissolving client resistance to working cooperatively in "here-and-now" focused, psychodynamically oriented therapy groups (Goldberg, 1981).

A twenty-six-year-old social worker, a client in a private practice group, had for two years after leaving graduate school been unable to submit her resumé in applying for jobs. She expressed the fear that other applicants were better qualified than she. Her obsession about her inability to get a job rendered her tense and restless. She had considerable difficulty falling asleep. Her considerable anxiety and exhaustion during group sessions evoked concern and much pseudofelicitousness and useless advice from the other group members. The advice-giving also "violated" a group norm of dealing with each of the group members where they were with each other in the immediate group situation, rather than discussing how group members might better regulate their lives while outside the group.

In clinical situations as described above, I have found paradoxical "homework" assignments to be excellent ways of using client symptoms to get the client to work on their avoidances outside the group. The paradoxical practitioner utilizes these assignments to enable the individual members of a therapeutic group to bring their conflictive issues, particularly those that attempt to manipulate the therapist into giving them advice and individual attention (thereby avoiding peer influence and peer struggles), into a perspective in which the client needs to question his or her assumptions.

The therapist recommended that before the client could allow herself to fall asleep she must first count resumés, similar to the palliative of counting sheep. Most importantly, however, the client was to give each of the resumés in her dream a title, that is to say, a reason for not being submitted for job application. Thus, for example, the first resumé: "My resumé is not as good as that of other candidates for the following reasons..." Resumé two: "Other candidates are better qualified because..." and so forth. The client reported that she never went past nine resumés without falling soundly asleep. My understanding of the dynamics involved in her situation was that she was obsessive about her fears without directly experiencing what she feared. By naming her fears she brought them to a more conscious level, which in subsequent sessions she explored with the group in terms of her competitiveness and jealousy with the other group members and the two co-therapists.

A second client with a sleep problem who had several years of individual psychotherapy was referred to a group. She agreed to join but indicated in the group sessions that she was misunderstood by the group members because her Southern upbringing was so different than the others in the group. She claimed that only the therapist could help her. He agreed. She was told to count sheep—pure, white, virgin sheep—and as each leapt over the fence they would encounter a large dirty muddy puddle into which they proceeded to fall. The client reported that she would just begin to fall asleep as the sheep went over the fence, but when they fell into the muddy puddle, she laughed so hard that she woke herself up. However, she got the point and began to work somewhat more trustingly and cooperatively in the group after the assignment. A twenty-five-year-old businessman who had an investment in not getting help for his anxieties repeatedly pointed out to the other participants and the therapist that they had not helped him in his year in the group. The therapist agreed with him and indicated that he finally understood why the client was getting no help. The therapist now realized that the client's problem was not that he was feeling anxious, but rather that he was not anxious enough. He was encouraged to store up his anxieties for the group sessions (that is, not allow himself to get anxious outside the group) and then to get as anxious as he could in the sessions and decisively demonstrate that the group members could not be helpful to him. What happened, of course, was that the client began to disclose to the group feelings that previously he tried to assuage by repressive-inspirational means by himself outside the group.

In that my space is limited I cannot describe here the innumerable other ways of using paradoxical interventions as an adjunctive approach in group psychotherapy. The interested reader is referred to a work in progress (Goldberg, in preparation).

Despite its wide application in dyadic treatment there is a surprising paucity of description in the literature of the use of paradoxical intervention as a primary approach in group psychotherapy. Two exceptions to this statement are the reports of Ormont (1974) and Spotnitz (1976) of their work with analytically oriented therapeutic groups.

I will in this chapter first discuss the rationale for paradoxical interventions of Ormont and Spotnitz. In that I differ in several respects from these authors' orientation, I will next describe the application of paradoxical intervention in two clinical situations in terms of my own therapeutic rationale.

The Work of Ormont and Spotnitz

Both Ormont and Spotnitz operate from a psychoanalytic base. They diagnose each of their group participant's refractory efforts at eliciting psychologically relevant information about themselves in terms of its level of psychosexual development. As such, resistive patterns formulated from birth to the age of two are referred to as "pre-oedipal resistance"; whereas resistive patterns developed between the ages of two and six are labeled "oedipal resistance." A preponderance of pre-oedipal or oedipal resistive patterns of individual patient reactions in a particular phase of a group would earn that group the appellation of being in the pre-oedipal or oedipal state. According to Ormont (1974) oedipal resistances respond to interpretative intervention by the therapist:

> Simply pointing out to a group in the Oedipal state that they are chit-chatting in order to avoid talking about their feelings toward each other is generally enough to set the members on the road toward resolving the resistance.

Pre-oedipal resistive patterns, on the other hand, for the most part

> will not respond to any intervention except reflective communications, sometimes called siding or joining. Unless the analyst joins pre-oedipal communications in such cases, these members will not be able to escape the repetitive patterns in which they are trapped and stalemated. As long as they are bound up with repressed aggression, they will be unable to describe the variety of feelings or the diversity of unverbalized thoughts within themselves. [Ormont, 1974]

Indeed, as Spotnitz (1976) states, the therapist's role during pre-oedipal resistance is not only to reflect residue tensions of the group members but to actually foster aggressive feelings in the group members:

> Urgent attention is given to resistance patterns that obstruct the verbalization of frustration-aggression. No attempt is made to demolish such pattern; [furthermore] [n]egative transference is fostered in a way that makes it possible to deal therapeutically with the problem of aggression, that is, by giving minimal directions and explanations and generally maintaining a reserved attitude. . . . The relative sparsity of the therapist's communications discourages the development of a positive-transference climate in which patients tend to bottle up anger. [P. 70]

I have been a participant in several professional workshops given by each of these clever and able practitioners in which they employed paradoxical interventions. From this experience and my own clinical and teaching experience of other group therapists, I find several major problems with viewing and treating the resistive patterns of groups in terms of the psychosexual development and the unexpressed anger of its members. I have found it more useful to regard these resistive patterns in terms of salient normative factors in the development of responsibility of the group members as a group. The witty, sarcastic provocateur role exemplified by Ormont and Spotnitz in the workshops I attended riveted the attention of the group members to the group leader's presence. The group members seemed unwilling to disengage from foil and banter with the group leader in order to attend to the resources of the other group participants. Utilizing paradoxical interventions with the wit and cleverness of an Ormont or Spotnitz appears to foster a leader, rather than group-centered focus. Undoubtedly few group members feel they have the resources to compete with or to contribute as prolifically as the group leader. Concomitantly, the group leader may become intoxicated by the admiration his wit and cleverness engender and, as such, be unwilling to confront those serious countertransferential issues which are colluding with the group members' resistive patterns. This collusion mitigates against effective therapeutic experience in that it is the group members, themselves, rather than the therapist who more frequently are the most salient therapeutic forces in the group (Goldberg, 1975).

"Rules" in Group Psychotherapy

The practice of contemporary group psychotherapy, as exemplified in the writings of such authors as Whitaker and Lieberman (1967), Yalom (1970), and Goldberg (1973, 1977[a]), emphasizes the salience of understanding the therapeutic group's normative structure in dealing efficaciously with individual and groupwide resistance. These normative structures will be referred to simply as "rules" in this chapter. For purposes of this chapter, rules will be operationally defined as "the latitudes of acceptable and rejectionable behavior group members implicitly agree to maintain in dealing with their uncertainty about how to proceed and how to make meaning of their presence in a therapy group." The rules being discussed become integral to the transactions of the group members. Moreover, the group members inveritably try, frequently with remarkable success, to impose these rules on the role and behavior of the group therapist. In this endeavor they try to induce the therapist to abandon or to not take seriously his chosen therapeutic role (Strean, 1964). As such, these subtle and implicit rules frequently mitigate against the meaningful processing and inculcation of insightful and potentially emotionally enriching transactions in a therapeutic group.

The work of George and Vasso Vassiliou (1976) suggests that mitigation against meaningful therapeutic endeavor stems from the therapist permitting the group members to decide for themselves what is therapeutically profitable group behavior *after* they have begun to violate the contract they have made with the therapist and other group members. The Vassilious indicate that group participants "attempt, and at times succeed, in nullifying their progress by intimating therapists with protests that they violate their 'human rights' when they try simply to stay firmly within the terms of the contract."

The Vassilious have recommended that when such group resistive patterns develop the therapist judiciously introduce disequilibrium producing interventions, such as the use of the "waking dream" and motor and graphic assignments during group sessions, in addition to startling and paradoxically expressed verbal statements, to dissolve the resistive pattens to productive group functioning.

A Rationale for Parodoxical Intervention in Group Psychotherapy

The task for the group practitioner who utilizes paradoxical interventions is to employ this approach to free up the facilitative energies and psychological resources of the peers, rather than fostering a leader-centered focus. For this to happen, paradoxical interventions should not be used whimsically and at random but must bear upon the contractual issues in the clients' relationship with the therapist that are still implicit and prevent open negotiation among them. Paradoxical strategies are reserved for those impasses in the group in which the group members have ceased functioning cooperatively with each other. Moreover, other therapeutic methods generally should be ruled out before considering indirect approaches such as paradoxical intervention (Ormont, 1974).

Clinical Illustrations of Paradoxical Intervention in Group Psychotherapy

This section describes the use of paradoxical interventions in two clinical situations. The interventions were directed toward groupwide resistance patterns. The clinical material is derived from the author's supervision of group psychotherapists in two different group-therapy training institutes. In the clinical cases to be discussed, suggestions were made to the therapists in training that would enable them to deal with their countertransferential issues, which were preventing them from moving away from the group members' leader-centered focus to that of the group participants taking responsibility for their conduct in the group.

In the first situation, a therapist in supervision discussed his adolescent group from a residential treatment school. His report suggested that the adolescents had made an implicit rule in the group not to take things seriously, to abort emotional self-disclosure. As a result, conflictive issues group members harbored were not probed and resolved. The group members, it appeared, were setting up the therapist as a surrogate parent who was required to control them, as exemplfied by their constant horseplay,—throwing objects around the room, hitting and poking one another, hiding under the desk and chairs. The therapist, fearful that the staff of the school would view the lack of discipline in the group as his inability fo keep things under control, attempted to impose his own rules against acting out in the group. The group members generally ignored these rules. In terms of value systems the situation could be viewed as follows: Because the therapist refused to "permit" the adolescents to conduct themselves in a way he regarded as "dysfunctional" he was reinforcing their irresponsibility—evidenced by their continuing to act out. In the supervisor's view a countertransferential issue was blocking progress in the group. The question being posed for the therapist was: "What kind of parent was he willing to be?" The adolescents were directing the therapist to be the kind of parent they experienced themselves as needing—was this the kind of parent the therapist wanted to be? The supervisor put this question to him. He replied that it wasn't. He was encouraged to give the group members the permission to take full responsibility for the rules they had made. In a subsequent session he said to the group members:

> "You have made a rule in here, as I understand it, that there will be no serious discussion—therefore, if you take seriously the rules you have established, I would expect someone in the group to cut off the discussion if someone else gets too serious."

In reply to their startled silence, he queried the group:

> "These are the rules you have created and have been living by; are these the rules you wish to continue to live by now that you have realized that you, yourselves, have created them, rather than they having been imposed upon you by someone else?"

In this example the therapist is using a paradoxical intervention which Watzlawick, et al. (1974) refer to as a *positioning* paradox, "the therapist attempts to shift a problematic 'position'—usually an assertion that the patient is making about himself or his problem—by accepting and exaggerating that position" (Rohrbaugh, et al., 1977).

In a second clinical example, two co-therapists in supervision reported that the patients in their adult out-patient clinic group in a private psychiatric hospital had been asking with some insistence that the therapist convert the therapeutic agenda of the group into a social arrangement. The group members maintained that they needed social experience more than they did psychotherapy. They maintained that if they had better social relationships, for example, more close friends, then they would not need further therapy. Several of the patients had confessed to the therapists that they have met together outside of the group. This activity had been happening more frequently in the last couple of months. The therapists had been careful to neither condone nor to tell the group members to cease their extragroup meetings. They felt uneasy about the outside meetings, however, particularly since they had learned that a married male and a married female group member had begun a relationship apart from the extra group meetings. The therapists viewed the patients in this group as passively manipulative, expecting the therapists to either comply with their social agenda or forcefully control their behavior by making rules prohibiting their outside meetings. The therapists were aware that if they complied with the second demand that several group members would drop out of the group. Earlier in supervision the co-therapists were asked to tape record the sessions for supervision. They hadn't done so prior to the supervision session being discussed here. Upon exploration of this issue they disclosed that they would feel rather embarrassed if they were to tape sessions. They feared that they would lose face as authorities in the group, who knew what they were doing, if they had to explain to their patients that their group work was being supervised. Thus, although the supervisees maintained that their major group objective was to enable the group members to take responsibility for their behavior in the group, they were unwittingly colluding with the group members' dependency needs by silently implying that they had knowledge and resources that might free up the patients to take seriously their therapeutic role, but that they were unexplainably withholding. Ostensibly the therapists tried to avoid being the judgmental and depriving surrogate parents the group members were trying to impress upon them, by not complying with their demands to be either condoning or prohibiting of their acting out. But in so doing they were experienced by the group members as witholding and depriving them of their expertise. This, in fact, was accurate. To break this therapeutic impasse, the therapists were told in supervision that it would be therapeutically useful if they regarded and acted as if their patients were responsible adults. They might convey to the group members, similar to the first group discussed, that they expected the group members to take responsibility for the rules they, themselves, had established. As the supervisees read the group members' behavior, the patients had made an implicit rule not to scrutinize their own personal begavior but rather to enact (act out) behaviors that would enable them not to have to think about unpleasant things. If this avoidance behavior weren't always successful, then the second group rule was that others in the group were to give them excellent but unacceptable advice. The third group rule, the supervisees became aware, was that the person who is given advice should profusely thank the others for their help and then promptly ignore it. Because these rules were in existence, the therapists were encouraged to indicate to the group members that the therapists assumed that the group members were acting in their own best interests. If they made such rules there must be good reason for doing so. The therapists were to convey their confidence that as responsible adults, the group members were expected to fully live up to the rules they had created. The supervisor's rationale could be summarized as follows: as long as the therapists were cast in and they, themselves, accepted the role of judgmental parental supervisors of the group members' dysfunctional rules (even though their judgmental processing was ostensibly silent), the patients did not have to create functional rules in which to deal with their pressing concerns. The group members tacitly assumed that their therapists would scrutinize and take proper care of them whenever they were childish and irresponsible. If, on the other hand, the therapists gave them "permission" for rebelling (creating rules to avoid therapeutic work), the group members would have to live by their own rules and would subsequently need to be more discerning about the rules they created for themselves. I have found that it is useful to support the validity of a paradox by combining it with other concerns that have been avoided being dealt with by either or both therapist and patient. In this instance it was the supervisees' failing to record their sessions. The supervisor suggested that the taping of sessions be explained to the group in the following fashion: that since the therapists were responsible professionals, they were checking out with their colleagues how they were conducting themselves with this group. They were told to subsequently come back to the group and report that their colleagues had agreed with them that the patients in this group were evidently responsible adults who should therefore have to live by their own rules.

The therapists reported that they had stated to the group in a succeeding session that they, the co-therapists, felt that the group members should not spend too much time exploring the issue of a group member who was leaving the group, because, from what the group members had been reporting to one another, getting involved in this kind of issue was upsetting. According to the rules of the group, members were not supposed to get too upset in the group. After all, they entered therapy because they were too easily agitated. Several of the group members verbally exploded at this absurd statement. They professed that the therapist's insinuation about their not being supposed to work on heavy emotional issues was a distortion of what they were trying to accomplish. Serious therapeutic work commenced for the first time in the group. The paradoxical intervention suggested by the supervisor and improvised upon by the supervisees is an illustration of what Haley (1963) has called a *prescribing* paradox. In this approach the therapist enables the patients to experience the implications of their dysfunctional behavior by suggesting that they continue to behave in such a way that they feel compelled to rebel against his permission. In short, the therapist encourages the patients to continue behaviors that he expects to be eliminated.

Too frequently conventional psychotherapeutic approaches recreate the same dysfunctional impasse which the client has repeatedly experienced as either "caving in" and surrendering to the power of the external agent and feeling worthless and self-denigrative as a result, or stubbornly resisting the intrusion and the potential enabling resources offered by the external agent. This is valid to the extent that the client experiences no other choice because he is continually presented with the same logical perspective of either/or. Paradoxical approaches, similar to the Eastern worldview, dispel this logical schism, refusing to reduce human experience to one or a few "real" motives or operating dynamics.

The therapeutic strategies employed in both supervisory situations serve to dissipate externalization of symptoms by the patients from whom they are directed. The paradox of "going with the resistance" exemplified in these two clinical cases gives permission to the group members to rebel against the therapist as an authority surrogate—divesting the acting out of rebeling value. This is to say, these strategies place each patient as "rebel" in a therapeutically valuable quandry: if he accepts the surrogate's permission to rebel against him as a depriving authority figure, he cannot reasonably continue to regard him as depriving. If he does not accept the permission to rebel against the therapist, he can no longer reasonably regard the therapist as an authority. This deprives the patient of a viable external object upon which to project his inner turmoil about feelings about himself which are ambivalent and conflicting. Because he is "free" to do what he claims he wishes, he must, then, take responsibility for the consequences of his actions. He must be more discerning, not so much in terms of what others ostensibly *tell* him about how he is to behave, but in fact how others subtly influence him and how, in turn, he affects others' actions. The neutralization of the external object as a target for externalizing feelings against mandatory behavior, therefore, forces the "rebel" to refocus on his inner conflicts and seek relief from his group mates and therapist in ways he could avoid in the past by externalizing his feelings of deprivation.

In short, by focusing on the group members' rules (norms), the therapist is able to carry out several important group functions: (1) he is able to separate his own values from that of the group members' projective identifications; (2) he is able to role-model a serious and responsible parental surrogate; (3) he is able to convey permissiveness, but only to the extent that the group members attend their endeavors responsibly; (4) he is able to maintain a group-centered focus, fostering the resources of peer influence.

The Use and Limitation of Paradoxical Approaches in Group Psychotherapy

The use of paradoxical intervention as described in this chapter is a powerful and frequently effective way of enabling participants in a therapeutic group to realize the impact of the psychosocial influences (norms or rules) on the ways they transact in a group; that is, how they are unwittingly permitted to act or how they are unwittingly enabled to avoid dealing with crucial concerns to them in the group. This is analogous to dyadic psychotherapy, in which the therapist reveals the intrapsychic influences on the client's behavior. Just as the individual is captive to his own unconscious strivings, so are members of a group captive—to the extent they are unaware of the psychosocial rules they have unwittingly fostered and implicitly agreed to maintain in dealing with their assumptions about themselves and those with whom they significantly interact.

The use of paradoxical intervention is an indirect way of influencing clients. As Rabkin (1977) indicates:

> At the present time no clear-cut guidelines can be offered about when to use a direct or an indirect approach. The choice depends both on the therapist's personal style and preferences, and on the type of patient and problem he is called upon to treat. [P. 69]

In this author's view, paradoxical interventions are generally ineffective and even deleterious unless dealing essentially with contractual disputes—that is, disagreements as to how therapist and client are to work together as responsible partners in the group (Goldberg, 1977[a]). Consequently, it is especially useful in dealing with groupwide resistance and when the therapist finds himself colluding with dysfunctional group norms. But the practitioner must keep in mind that the use of any single paradoxical intervention is rarely effective by itself.[3] Paradoxical strategies need to be combined with other therapeutic strategies and, most of all, with clinical sensitivity and intuition.

The Utilization of Paradoxical Approaches As a Way of Being

All systems of psychotherapy and psychosocial education seem to share in common the aim of increasing the participant's choices in the conduct of his life. Each person experiences a choice of how much of himself he is willing to experience deeply. Experiencing the deeper recess of one's self is frequently painful, as it reveals unbuttressed the loneliness and dread our ontological responsibility in a world of uncertainty evokes. The defenses we erect, which may be perceived as admirable personality traits by ourselves and/or others, provide a respite from pain insofar as the probe of our deeper concerns is averted. *Man's basic choice is one of choosing how he wishes to experience life* (Goldberg, 1973). This rationale has important implications for two important clinical phenomena: "resistance" and "psychosis."

Psychiatry's notion of resistance is predicated on the assumption that "something is happening" and it is being avoided rather, than the possibility that many things in the person are happening and that none of these is necessarily more important than any other. Psychiatric reductionism, then mitigates against seeing manifold possibility where each is a viable possibility—an option—which has its consequences, whether recognized and followed, or ignored or denied.

"Craziness" is the constraint of a logical, rational worldview on a Self, which precludes the Self's own idiosyncratic view by imposing the insistence that either the Self's world view is invalid, that he is at odds and divergent with everyone else, or that if the Self's view is valid, then everyone in the world is mad. The Self is given the choice of correctness and isolation or invalidity and human company. Most people, as the character of Celia in T. S. Eliot's play tells us, prefer not to hold on to their idiosyncratic (or narcissistic) world view if it means losing human company.[4] Celia says:

> But first I must tell you that I should really like to think that there's something wrong with me.... Because if there isn't then there's something wrong or at least, very different from what it seems to be with the world itself.... and that's much more frightening! That would be terrible. So I'd rather believe there is something wrong with me, that could be put right. I'd do anything you told me, to get back to normality.

Paradoxical Search Into Self

I have conducted professional workshops that seek to uncover the participants' basic choices in how he has chosen to experience himself-in-the-world. Some of these exercises—or simulated existential situations—are described in Appendix C of this book so that the reader may purvey them for his own edification. I will limit myself to an illustration from a workshop of one of these exercises, "The Potlatch Ceremony." Workshop descriptions of some of the other exercises are contained in a previous book (see Goldberg, 1977[a]).

For purposes of a workshop concerned with paradox, the Potlatch Ceremony has intriguing possibilities. I ask each of the participants to think about and then select that aspect of himself—that personality trait or feature—that other people admire most about him and then symbolically toss that trait into an imaginary bonfire in the middle of the group. The notion behind this symbolic gesture is that for purposes of the exercise, the participant has "disowned" this attribute and its implications for his behavior.

Each of the participants is then asked to describe how they feel about themselves, now that they have cast aside what may be regarded as a vital component of their personal functioning. In a two-day professional training institute for group therapists, a timid young social worker, who had been struggling for two days with getting in touch with deep-seated resentment and anger, asked the two group leaders and the other participants in the group for permission to be assertive. She asked to disown her cooperative and placating demeanor. One of the leaders and the other participants readily agreed. The other leader, instead of agreeing, suggested that she verbally go around the group and ask directly of each participant for their permission to be assertive. Each again readily agreed. She smiled, unwittingly successful in avoiding conflict in "becoming more aggressive." When she came to the second leader, he said, "You don't need my permission to be either assertive or angry, but if you're asking for my permission, you can be angry with anyone you want to in the group, but not with me. You don't have my permission to be angry with me!" The group leader had imposed a paradoxic dilemma for the participant within the context of the Potlatch Exercise. The social worker was forced at that moment in time to face squarely that she was asking for the appearance but not the substance of responsibility as an autonomous adult. Here, as in other instances in her life, she required the protective goodwill of others, so as not to have to experience directly her aloneness and separation from others.

In employing the Potlatch Exercise with therapeutic groups, I further suggest that they continue this "as if" stance outside the group and report the results back to the group.

Chapter Nine

Creating Meaning in Psychotherapy

" . . . that which we are, we are—one equal temper of heroic hearts, Made weak by time and fate, but strong in will To strive, to seek, to find, and not to yield."
—Alfred Tennyson

I have reiterated throughout this volume that man craves a sense of meaning to his existence. Man, the emotional and passionate creature—which he often hides from his own awareness—in finding himself in an indifferent world, seeks concern and reciprocity with his fellow creatures.

It is my contention that if psychotherapy is to have a continuous and growthful propensity, it must be involved with the creation of meaning for the client. The client entering therapy suffers from an inability to address adequately his existential responsibility. It is his ontological obligation to give some direction to his own existence. Without this direction, a person suffers from a lack of experienced meaning in his existence. His suffering is exacerbated by the therapist's collusion in avoiding addressing these concerns in their encounter together (Goldberg, 1977[a]).

What does this perspective have to do with the reports of the effectiveness of nonpsychodynamic psychological treatment? Many experts claim, with impressive empirical evidence, that the method of dealing with emotional distress by probing the normally hidden contents of the mind no longer has relevance in an era of rapidly changing beliefs about what emotional disturbance is all about. Researchers have found, for example, that as they have unraveled more and more the mysteries of the brain, severe mental disturbance, such as chronic depression or schizophrenia, derives from chemical rather than psychological imbalances. As a result of these findings, powerful new drugs have been developed to treat a great many emotional problems successfully. As for the less severely disturbed, there is an increasing number of sex counselors, behavior therapists, biofeedback technicians, meditation guides, hypnosis mentors and encounter group leaders toward which to turn. There has been even a reluctant but noticeable acceptance among psychoanalysts concerning the efficacy of some of these modalities. There also appears to be impressive evidence that cognitive interpretation is insufficient, frequently insignificant, in psychological amelioration. For example, the first controlled study comparing behavioral modification techniques with drugs as methods of achieving weight-loss has found not only that those subjects using behavioral techniques do better over a long period of time, but also that subjects using only behavior modification do better than subjects combining the psychological techniques with drugs. Moreover, even in instances where psychodynamic methods are involved in what appears to be successful amelioration, the emphasis on the "correctness" of cognitive interpretations must be questioned, in that various psychodynamic therapies based upon differing ontological assumptions seem to be generally of similar effectiveness.

This state of affairs suggests to me that the various facets of psychological treatment lack a coherent and integrative concept(s) to explain the phenomenon of psychological amelioration. This state of affairs is both paradoxical and ironic, since it is my contention that the concept required in this endeavor is that of meaning and purpose.

The importance of the quest for meaning is a neglected issue in the psychological literature. Indeed, in keeping with psychological reductionism, all attempts at meaning in psychotherapy are regarded, most particularly in psychoanalysis, as rationalizations of uneasy instincts and relegated to the status of a subliminated endeavor.

In my view, the quest for meaning in human existence through therapeutic encounter and client-therapist collaboration endeavors are joined. Therapists who equate freedom and autonomy tend to ignore interpersonal partnership as central to the therapeutic encounter, for if man is an autonomous agent he must then free his solitary will, as encounter, EST, Gestalt practitioners among others, exhort him to assert himself in seeking happiness, meaning, and security (Linthorst, 1975). In my contrasting view, the journey into Self requires the presence of another. We come to know ourselves through the other. Hora (1975) points out

> communion is that union which makes differentiation possible. Man becomes an individual through participation. [P. 146]

The journey into Self is most productive in a climate in which each partner is in the process of seeking an increased awareness of his own identity and is free to disengage from relationships in which his or her happiness and productivity are dependent upon the feelings and regard of the other. Each of the Selves on this journey needs to seek to explore, experience, and hopefully come to terms with some of the contradictory attitudes, assumptions, and paradoxical ways of being each has defined for himself and has allowed others to impose upon him, in avoiding becoming that which he seeks to be. Rather than focusing on changing these ways of being—trying to become something or someone else—each needs to explore the fulfillment of these paradoxical and avoided behaviors in encouraging each other to become what they are. The cogent "paradox" this journey attempts to address is how each participant may retain and fulfill his own individuality, while at the same time being a functioning partner in an interrelating interpersonal unit. I have written this volume as a guide for myself in this journey in search of Self. This chapter is devoted to a quest in psychotherapy for meaning in consort.

The demands of a meaningful psychotherapy that meets the requirements of the creative self are predicated upon the full recognition and articulation of an ontological view of man, in which the values of the practitioner are directly acknowledged and testable within the experiences of those with whom he works.

Since professionalism and alleged expertise contribute to the fragmentation and illusions of prevailing psychotherapies, a meaningful psychotherapy needs to divest its practitioners of their phony baggage. In this system the practitioner is free to represent himself in all his aspects of Self, rather than be confined to a few professional attributes. This may be appreciated in terms of the massive but generally unrecognized investment practitioners have in keeping their clients victims. Illustratively, I have been criticized for my view of the freedom of human will (Goldberg, 1977[b]) discussed in chapter four. It has been argued by some of my colleagues that if man is truly free, then science as a descriptive discipline that seeks to recognize man's lawfulness must be abandoned. Psychotherapies which are regarded as emanations of science must likewise be jettisoned. That this argument does not logically follow my exposition and is clearly specious, was of far less concern to me than the implications for the victimization of clients. Personally, I experienced these criticisms not so much as attacks on what my critics regarded as the invalidity of my presentation[1] of human freedom, but their own sadness and despair in losing their roles as experts (healers) in regard to victims of predictable ailments. What these critics seem to be saying was: "Alas, if man is really free, then who am I? However, if man is a victim, then I have an identity as his healer!"

I, on the other hand, experience freedom quite differently. I can be no more liberated than I permit others to be. To constrain another with my illusion and my tyranny of beliefs about him, to that extent I invest my energy and my freedom in that constraint. Furthermore, I have less freedom to be who I am, because I have diminished the other Self's experience of freedom to see me as he might see me, not as I will be seen. Only to the extent that I permit another to see me as he will see me, can I see myself as I intend.

The creation of meaning in psychotherapy comes from the therapist treating himself and expecting the client to treat him on the basis of what he is enacting in therapy, rather than as he believes he should or wants to be treated. Too frequently, as Shepard (1970) indicates, the client's concerns are

> met with the rejoinder: "Why do you ask?" This very response often contains the answer within. It indicates that the therapist is an excessive game-player—someone who is afraid to reveal the person behind the professional façade, someone who would rather joust verbally than deal directly with vital and pressing concerns. [P. 9]

Unless the therapist provides something that enables the client to be as the client intends or is freed up to be, then he cannot expect respect or commitment. (This was discussed in chapter eight.) The creation of meaning comes from what one *does,* not from morality—one's good character and good intentions.

Therapeutic Partnership As a Journey Into Self

To offer the client relevant information about how I experience him, I must allow myself to experience freely. When experiencing freely, I tend to experience the encounter situation more emotionally than when feeling comfortable. I experience choking up, giddiness, irritation, anxiety, sensuality, and other emotional reactions that are apperceptively filtered out by my more clinical and "professional" formulations and notions of certainty about what I should be attending to in a therapeutic encounter. It is only from an immediate and continuing commitment to the real possibility of a relationship with the person with whom I am involved in an encounter—a commitment that is not bracketed off by oaths of conduct, statements of clinical interest and responsibility for the other, rather than responsibility for my own intentionality—that I am aware of a deep sadness and personal loss from our separation in the world. The closer we come together, the more we are aware of our separation. The more we get in touch with the ultimate estrangement, the more we can appreciate what we are currently sharing together and the preciousness of the present moment.

In enduring a risky ordeal experienced together, people come to truly know one another and develop, as a result, a genuine liking and respect for one another. At the moment we lose the sense of certainty and security provided by theoretical and clinical procedure, so that we can no longer predict the outcome of our being together, the possibility of a meaningful encounter lies before us. It is to the degree that the client senses, as the relationship manifests it, that the practitioner is willing and able to negotiate how the client is to be regarded and treated, that both agents within an encounter can cast aside reactive fears and the need for safety, and can accommodate to each other. In so doing, each in exploring their interpersonal situation, comes to experience himself and the other with increased meaningfulness.

The journey into Self, as I have said, requires the presence of another. We come to know ourselves through the other. The journey in quest of meaning is, in my view, most productive in a setting in which each agent seeks an increased awareness of his own identity (Goldberg, 1977a). The habit of denying one's own values while functioning as a therapist becomes resistantly entrenched in most practitioners. They have been led to believe, from their training and from reports in the literature of other practitioners, that the responsible practitioner should not want anything for himself other than to be fairly remunerated. He should only be there to deal with how the client wishes to be. For many practitioners, the exploration of the practitioner's being-in-the-world within the therapeutic encounter is an unconscionable endeavor, as if the practitioner were without existential anxiety and concern that might be decisively shaping the encounter. Practitioners often do quite some number on themselves and their clients in maintaining this duplicity. Groesbeek and Taylor (1977) suggest that in the modern psychological representation of the myth of *Asclepins,* the patient in psychotherapy has a healer within himself and the therapist has a patient within himself. Each agent in a therapeutic encounter must accommodate his unconscious projection to the needs of the other if real healing is to occur. The therapist in this sense must be prepared to have his own inner wounds activated in therapy. In this endeavor, he may be able to heal the client and give meaning to his own distress.

For the client to become a more responsible and effective person, he needs to be given responsibility for collaborating in his own emotional growth. This endeavor requires a partnership between therapist and client. The practitioner serves as a role model. The client will be no more willing to struggle for meaning in his journey into Self than he senses the practitioner is in his own personal and interpersonal journeys. As such, psychotherapeutic practice requires a rationale and a methodology that are based upon a realistic assessment of the ontological conditions in the therapeutic encounter. This rationale and methodology must enable the practitioner to get in touch with his own, as well as his client's, loneliness and despair, to address the conditions that present themselves in a therapeutic encounter in which the therapist and client take each other seriously. To the extent that a practitioner does not consciously experience his struggle with his own humanity in his encounter with a client, he tends to regard the therapeutic relationship as a function. The therapeutic relationship under these conditions becomes an abstraction, appropriate for description and convenient for observation, but at the same time unavailable as a meaningful human experience in which client and therapist share concerns in regard to their being-in-the-world (Goldberg, 1977[a]). Issues of existential concern are denied in a setting in which the therapist suppresses his own intentionality. I am in agreement with Hugh Mullan (1955) that therapists frequently impose ritualistic requirements—for example, not speaking until the client has, answering a question with a question, or leaving unclarified the statements the client makes about the "nontherapy"-related aspects of the practitioner's life—supposedly for the benefit of the client, to promote his "cure," but they are actually a means for the therapist to avoid his own anxiety about the common struggle he shares with his client in their mutual quest for their own humanity.

Jules Older, a New Zealand psychologist, has discussed the conditions that when absent in psychotherapy limit the success of the therapeutic endeavor. According to Older (1977), there are four current taboos that may contribute to failure in psychotherapy. These taboos are against touching, embarrassment, noisy emotions, and long individual sessions. Older argues that by forbidding direct physical contact with those with whom we work, we have cut ourselves off, as practitioners, from very basic ways of relating and providing comfort to our clients. In some instances, Older indicates, it is the only way of reaching the client. Similarly, Older argues that quiet and rational discourse is frequently an avoidance of emotional concerns. Discussion of pain isn't necessarily the expression of hurt, but may be instead its avoidance. It may be inconvenient or difficult for a therapist to allow the expression of noisy emotions in his office, but getting in touch with deep hurt is indispensable to meaningful psychotherapy. When this hurt is experienced, it may emerge with considerable noisy release. Correspondingly, the avoidance of embarrassment in psychotherapy constitutes an implicit agreement between therapist and client to avoid troublesome and painful concerns. This pact may be firmly maintained for years. Older points out that the silent agreement not to discuss painful and embarrassing subjects reinforces the client's feeling of self-denigration and unacceptability that he brought with him into psychotherapy. "For if even the therapist, fully imbued with transference, omnipotence, and gratitude, can't talk about something, it must be awful, indeed" (Older, 1977). According to Older, prolonged sessions increase the likelihood of the intimacy experienced in therapeutic encounter dissolving the taboos against noisy emotions, discussing embarrasing concerns, and physical touch. It is Older's practice to maintain individual sessions as long as necessary to work through the emotional crisis.

The Therapist's Creative Self

To move psychotherapy from simply a curative system to one of proactive growth and personal development, the therapist must be willing and able to use his Self creatively. He must be able to dream and dare to express and emotionally enact what his client dare not even imagine. The therapist must sense and participate in the client's experience not *as if,* but *as* a real person—fully letting himself go—well almost, with the only reserve being a potent sense that when he experiences a hesitation in himself or a limitation in his own or his client's participation in their emotive enactment of their being together in encounter, he will respect the hesitation or sense of limitation and despite any deep sadness of holding back from full participation with his client, seek to come to understand the source and consequences of that hesitation.

Perhaps before we get too immersed in the content and process of transforming psychotherapy into a more meaningful endeavor, we need to stand back for a moment and requestion its context and structure.

Giving Away Psychotherapy

Edgar Levenson (1972) in his critique on modern psychoanalysis has indicated that "psychoanalysis offers as little solace these days as reading Kierkegaard on one's deathbed. Once a potent force in the affairs of man, it seems in a fair way of going the road of religion and philosophy...." [p. 3].

Why has psychoanalysis, as well as other psychotherapies, fallen into discontent? Levenson points out:

It is clear that one cannot isolate psychoanalysis from its cultural context and study its development over the years as though it were a continuous phenomenon. The changes in psychoanalysis are discontinuous. When society changes, all these transformations shift, and the new system of relationships that emerges is not a lineal development from the past but a new arrangement. Our relationship to our patients may not be any more enlightened than was Freud's. . . . [P. 38]

The transformations in culture and society, particularly the pervasive sense of alienation and enervation of passion and commitment to other Selves, may require that we may no longer carry on "professional" psychotherapy but instead enact a dialogue between people, each having influences and impact on the other, each struggling to come to terms with his or her own human condition within their coming together.

In establishing a profession you erect a universe, a justification for that universe and a need to which the agents of that universe promote (Illich, 1976). Moreover, you foster a guilt among those in the general populace who you claim should be partaking of your services, because as in the case of psychotherapy, they are "not just right psychologically" without their course of treatment. Psychotherapists have become as William Shakespeare so cynically depicted the tradesman in the opening scene of *Julius Caesar*. In being asked by Flavius why he was not in his shop on a working day attending to his trade but was instead leading men around the streets, the tradesman replied: "Truly, sir, to wear out their shoes, to get myself more work . . . ."

Before there was psychotherapy as an establishment, people just took care of the needs for which psychotherapy has been erected. The establishment of psychotherapy also seriously mitigates against self-help. The psychotherapy I am proposing needs to look at the ways ("tools") to address the human condition—ways that are not treatment, problem-solving, helping, giving, or so forth. I am speaking rather of ways of being with myself and others that are more meaningful, gratifying, and enlightening than those that each of us typically allows ourselves. I assume that some of these ways of being have long ago been created, devised, or discovered, but have been discarded because they don't coincide with professional standards of psychotherapy practice. An example of this notion is several of the projects contained in the Appendix of this volume. One of the most interesting seekers of ancient wisdom was G.I. Gurdjieff (1979) who describes his meetings with men of wisdom in his autobiographic volume, *Meetings With Remarkable Men*.

In my view, more people should be treated with those skills we call "psychotherapeutic." We should regard this endeavor as an avocation, a life style, rather than a profession, and utilize these styles in our personal and social life rather than in the narrow circumscribed mystique of psychotherapy where only therapeutic relationships develop. I believe as gratituous as it may sound that those who are 'therapists' should seek their livelihood elsewhere, and when they "do psychotherapy," it should be with only a few people, without cost, as one volunteers his services and time out of care and concern for others, rather than out of his need to transact his business.

It is not that psychotherapists cannot and do not make a contribution to others, but that the establishment of psychotherapy as a profession frequently mitigates against the best of what psychotherapy can be. For example, it is hardly unusual for practitioners to treat fifteen or more people a day. Can they give each of these clients a genuine, meaningful human experience? Many practitioners claim that they derive considerable self-growth and other essential human enrichment for themselves by being therapists. Can they with any sense of integrity charge for giving a genuine human experience, especially when they admittedly are enriched by the experience themselves!

The creation of meaning in psychotherapy is posed by the mutual endeavor—responded to by both therapist and client—of what is the meaning of their being together, their encountering and relating to each other at this precise moment in their being-in-the-world. This concern, in each of its various forms, needs to be continually returned to in reflecting, projecting, and directing the therapeutic relationship. Without the continual awareness of this existential concern, therapy remains at the level of a mechanical symptom-directed endeavor (Goldberg, 1977[a]). The presenting complaint, the working alliance, the setting of treatment goals, and therapeutic contract need continually be processed in terms of this existential concern.

The Therapeutic Struggle

The Self has suffered narcissistic injury, accruing paradoxical power, in gaining control over its environment. In each Self's struggling to survive in the uncertain world in which it has found itself, it has acquired a personal sense of mastery and potence over the forces pressing against its existence. To a great extent, to master these forces it has surrendered its personal autonomy in identifying with a few specific caretakers and has, as a result, felt liberated from the constant battle with external forces. Hence, the individual has the untoward opportunity to experience the forces within himself cry out in indignation and despair at his lost power and autonomy. He can no longer avoid these fierce, uncertain forces within himself. For these forces have proven more resilient and fearsome than those of the natural world he gave up his personal power to master. He has, because external forces seem less onerous to deal with, projected these fears on to his caretakers. He has sensed, but could rarely articulate, the realization that by identifying with and being protected by caretakers, he has avoided the personal and natural struggle with his own existence, leaving himself feeling impotent and distrustful of himself.

This subtle but powerful interface of internalization and externalization of power relations has serious consequences for the therapeutic relationship. As such, I am interested in the dimension of power—why some men seize power and why others permit them to do so. When some stop short of remending a situation, they say in effect to others: "The situation is not serious or important enough to do more—anyone else who wishes to do so has my permission to do what he likes about the situation!"

The most malevolent, psychopathic men step in and take over at this juncture. He who does nothing to remedy a situation gives permission to others to continue things as they are. But as psychotherapists, we can hardly stand still with such a stolid attitude. We are obliged to take full cognizance of our own power relations and their implications in our struggles with our clients.

The struggle for meaning in psychotherapy is crystalized in the dimensions of power manifested in the therapeutic encounter (Goldberg, 1978[b]). This should not be an altogether surprising statement. It is the nature of human relations that people try to influence one another. Many of these endeavors are conducted in such a way that people can choose whether or not, and how, they will be influenced. In many other instances, however, people have little or no choice about the nature and impact of others' attempts to influence them. What about psychotherapy? As an influence process, is psychotherapy a democratic or egalitarian enterprise, as many of its practitioners claim? Are client and therapist struggles for control and power, therefore, essentially attributable to transference and countertransference distortion? Or are these struggles more frequently the *sine qua non* of interpersonal relations, without which psychotherapy would represent a pale imitation of social reality? Neither theorists nor practitioners of psychotherapy have given sufficient attention to the very salient dimension of therapist and client power struggles in psychotherapy. For the most part, power remains an unspoken dimension and issue in psychotherapy. (*Power* is operationally defined in this chapter as the capacity to control the actions of another person and to modify the other's sentiments and attitudes.)

Indeed, of all the concepts important to what transpires in a therapeutic relationship—not only to the agents directly involved in the immediate therapeutic situation, but also others in the client's social system—I can think of no other dimension that has been so neglected. It is not that we have not yet discovered the concept of power! There are a few practitioners, notably Szasz, Haley, and Halleck who have spoken forcefully to the issue. A rare exception to the paucity of theoretical delineation of power struggles in psychotherapy is the writing of Lawrence Friedman (1975). Therapists, generally, speak more freely about the sexual dimension in psychotherapy, than of their power struggles with clients. (Since sexual struggles are frequently related to power conflicts, I would suspect that power struggles are generally broached in the guise of other issues in psychotherapy.)

The great difficulty I had personally in acquiring acceptance for a workshop on the issue of power for American Psychological Association conventions and for other professional conferences highlights the denial of this issue's importance. Of further concern to me is that when the manifestations of power heavily intruded in professional workshops I have attended, the leaders have typically, in my view, anxiously dismissed the intrusion as an epiphenomenon or an analyzable countertransferential (or transferential) issue which was relegated to be dealt with in the participants' own personal therapy. I have described these experiences in a recent book (Goldberg, 1977ᵃ).

My research and my clinical experience as a practitioner and a psychotherapy educator have made it abundantly clear that, when we put aside the details of diverse theoretical positions, the common fulcrum of all therapeutic endeavor resides in the *struggle* (and frequently the conflict) between therapist and client—as to how meaningfully each will permit himself and the other to become in the therapeutic relationship. This struggle exists with even the most ostensibly willing and open clients. It is impossible to ignore with more recalcitrant clients. Indeed, if this struggle were not crucial to efficacious ameliorative endeavor, interactive immediacy between client and therapist would not be necessary. In that event, clients could be referred to the many fine books and audiotapes describing psychological development and proactive functioning. Yet, interestingly, this therapeutic struggle is not central to major theories of psychotherapy. Therapeutic resistance, whether regarded as residing in either the client or the therapist or (in a few theories) in the way they come together, is seen in psychotherapy theory as an intrusion—an interference in allowing the therapist to go about the business of proper therapeutic practice. These psychological theories, as a result, fail to consider therapeutic resistance as a product of the failure to adequately address crucial power struggles evoked by the ways both therapist and client come together to address their existential concerns. To the extent that current theories of psychotherapy deny the crucial importance of not only recognizing, but savoring, the struggle between therapist and client, they are insufficient for understanding meaningful therapeutic endeavor.

Meaningful therapeutic endeavor is integrally related to the quality of its emotional communication. Direct encounter is required in order to investigate the intricacies of human meaning and purpose through the expression of emotional communication. The very profound threats and demands of this endeavor set limits on the participants' particular expressiveness of their human condition in the therapeutic encounter. Communication in most therapeutic encounters, for example, is limited to the parameters of vocal and nonactive, tactile language. Sensual and active tactile expression is generally explicitly prohibited or anxiously avoided by the therapist and client. Restriction in the expression of emotional communication crystalizes the underlying conflict existent in every therapeutic encounter as to how therapist and client will address their personal concerns with each other. As I have already argued, the struggle between therapist and client is the focal issue in psychotherapy—awareness of this prevents the therapist from managing the lives of his clients and moving them to therapeutically logical conclusions that may be in contradiction with the existential conditions of his clients' existence. In literary form this existential struggle is poignantly portrayed in Pirandello's play, *Six Characters in Search of an Author.* The stage-manager finds that the personal conflict of the characters is unmanageable. He maintains that the six characters' expressions of their human condition will not neatly fit into a theatrical production. He demands that the characters refine and control their disturbance, so that each of their personal sagas can be harmoniously blended together in a drama he can then direct as a stage production.

The practitioner's therapeutic system, like the stage manager's style of direction, represents value-orientations as to how the practitioner requires his clients to address their human condition. Unless the practitioner is comfortable in exercising his considerable power in his clients' behalf, and unless this influence is openly explored with his clients, their work together will be replete with implicit, if not manifest, struggles of will and moral persuasion. The psychotherapist's power resides not in the validity of his explanations but in his audacity in being willing to—with the client's conviction or at least desperate need—reduce all matters of importance to psychological terms, which the therapist knows better than does the client. Consequently, the client need no longer be obliged to validate explanation in terms of his own experience.

In this enterprise, the only power left to the client as long as he remains in the therapeutic system—conceptual or real—is the utilization of *subversive power.* Each of us, as practitioners, has experienced our clients' subversive power—the various indirect strategies clients employ to negate our misdirected efforts to help them and/or to protect ourselves. Our clients deserve the opportunity to acquire more direct power than this!

To help us get beyond these therapeutic impasses, we need to appreciate the role of philosophical depression (which I have discussed earlier in this volume) in the therapeutic struggle. Philosophical depression is the narcissistic connection to therapeutic resistance. In giving in to external influences, be they therapeutic or not, the Self experiences a loss of meaning. Its alienation from others gives the Self a romantic, unique position. In giving in to object-influences, the Self is forced to recognize hope, the illusion of its tragic hero-character, and its commonality with other Selves. The therapist should not threaten this stance ("illusion"), but instead enable the client to retain his uniqueness, by the therapist's sharing his own sense and need for uniqueness and his own experience of the struggle of sharing his intentionality and the alienation, anguish, and dread he experiences in expressing this import to another Self. To share, to come together, must be explored in terms of its nuances, its continual choices of how much, how deeply, how lastingly, how involvingly the Self chooses to be moment-to-moment, so that no single redirection, no single veering from "basic choice" (choices from the past) need be experienced as giving up the Self's uniqueness and its meaning. Rather, this meaning can be broadened, intensified, contradicted, and redirected to come to a more profound emotional and intellectual awareness and appreciation of the meaning of the intentionality of the Self and the postures it assumes.

The crucial existential struggles I have been alluding to between client and therapist have to do with the interrelated questions of "How far do we go in trying to help others?" and "How do we go about trying to answer this concern for ourselves as practitioners and enable our clients to answer it with us in consort?"

The philosopher and sociologist Ivan Illich has rather thoughtfully examined these questions. He has persuasively argued that it is man's condition to suffer and this suffering is both necessary and an honorable part of each man's life. External attempts at amelioration of another man's suffering are, according to Illich, morally and psychologically disruptive. Therapists who specialize in "helping" their clients get in the way of understanding and dealing with their clients and their deeper concerns. They do not respect people as they are. Too frequently these practitioners don't know how to relate any other way. As Ronald Laing (1962) has so poignantly written:

> To be understood correctly is to be engulfed, to be smothered, to be enclosed, devoured, eaten up, stifled in or by another's all-embracing comprehension. It is lonely and painful to be always misunderstood, but there is at least from their point of view a measure of safety in isolation. [Pp. 41–69]

Each of us already knows all we need to know. The problem is to understand what we intuitively know by experiencing more fully what we are experiencing—to fully experience our passions. Left to his own devices, man will survive and heal himself. Enter the Doctor—God—and with him a galaxy of dependencies and untolerated ailments that only the Doctor can alleviate. The Doctor convinces man that he deserves a life without pain, and then sets himself up as the only profession capable of supplying man with that life (Illich, 1976).

In *The Lives of a Cell,* Dr. Lewis Thomas wrote that

> the great secret, known to internists and learned early in marriage by internists' wives, but still hidden from the general public, is that most things get better by themselves. Most things, in fact, are better by morning. [p. 85]

We have become accustomed to expecting, indeed demanding, instant relief from our ailments, our pains, our trepidations, and our doubts. Why wait until the morning when we have been repeatedly led to believe that prolonged suffering can generally be avoided! But what if Illich and Thomas are correct? The therapist who attempts to heal his client interferes with the client healing himself. Under the assumption that the therapist can no longer legitimately claim to be a healer, nor can validly insist that he is an expert in knowing objective reality or his client's subjective world, can he offer his client anything of value or must he be bound up forever in Dysart's obsessive-compulsive helplessness?

Clearly the practitioner shares with his client the ontological requirement to give some direction to his own existence. The therapist can enable his client to derive meaning from the client's struggles by offering him the courage he has found and the values he has derived in experiencing his own world and in struggling with the forces pressing upon his own human condition. If Dysart had regarded his own struggles, not as his weakness and his hypocrisy, but as the pangs of passion, caring, and concern, he would more likely have offered his client a meaningful therapeutic experience. Simultaneously, by freeing himself to discover the caring in his own despair, he might have found himself, and enabled his client to find value and meaning from his own suffering. Nietzsche told us as much:

> Physician, help yourself! Thus you help your patient, too. Let this be his best help that he may behold with his eyes the man who heals himself.

Dysart's countertransferential problem was not that he questioned his qualifications to practice psychiatry—as intimated by several psychiatric and theatre critics—but his unwillingness to acknowledge his feelings of compassion toward his client as a genuine statement of his capacity to care. Dysart's therapy (despite how the playwright presented it on stage) must ultimately prove futile. Dysart failed to permit his client's dilemma to challenge his own ontological struggles. As he was unwilling to allow his client to enter his own personal world, neither could he fully enter his client's world. Because Dysart feared passion, he could not fully participate with his client (nor his wife, nor anyone else for that matter!) What the therapist has to offer is his passion. Not its specifics—but its validity, its right to be for its own sake. For without passion there is no life. Dysart realized this, he tells us:

Real worship! Without worship you shrink, it's as brutal as that.... I shrank my *own* life. No one can do it for you. I settled for being pallid and provincial out of my own eternal timidity. [P. 95]

As in *Equus,* the effectiveness of the therapist who lives without passion must be critically questioned. Refusing to participate in the passions he is obsessive about, Dysart was unable to meaningfully articulate the fundamental concerns with which intellectually he was struggling. As Dysart's statements suggest, he is only able to speak about his "struggle," but not capable of speaking *from* the experience of that struggle.[1] Thus, his ontological questions are expressed with extreme vagueness:

questions I've avoided all my professional life.... I don't know. *And nor does anyone else.* Yet *if* I don't know—if I can never know that—then what am I doing here? I don't mean clinically doing or socially doing—I mean *fundamentally*! These questions, these whys are fundamental—yet they have no place in a consulting room. So then, do I? [P. 88]

Speaking from his own passion is required of the therapist, as the only expertise he can validly claim is creating consensus reality with his client—that is to say, negotiating and contracting with him in such a way that enables each to meaningfully experience the other's struggles with the assumptions the other Self holds about the world. Levinson (1972) argues:

The most loving act of the therapist is to be real, to be there and to permit himself the discomfort of engaging the patient's system. [P. 214]

In a word, the therapist must become part of the client's world in order to jointly re-create it. The creation of consensus reality is necessary to remove the mystique from the process of psychotherapy—to free both agents to assume their own humanity and to deal equitably with each other. To do so the therapist can no longer speak of other men's emotions. As Solomon (1977) poses:

A description of someone else's emotion is one thing; understanding one's own is something else. And our problem is to understand *for me (us),* subjectively, what it is to *have* an emotion. [P. 171]

An Investigation of

Chapter Ten

Masters of the

Therapeutic Arts

Marcellus: "But what trade art thou? Answer me directly."
Second
Commoner:"A trade, sir, that, I hope, I may use with a safe conscience; which is in-
deed, sir, a mender of bad soles."
Marcellus: "What trade, thou knave? Thou naughty knave, what trade?"
Second
Commoner:"Nay, I beseech you, sir, be not out with me. Yet, if you be out, sir, I
can mend you."
Marcellus: "What mean it thou by that? Mend me, thou saucy fellow."
—William Shakespeare, *Julius Caesar,* Act I, Scene I

I would like to share with the reader in this chapter an exciting research project I am currently engaged in concerned with the process of psychotherapy.

As practitioners who are involved in an applied art, rather than a legitimate scientific endeavor with coherent and validated psychological theory, we need to observe "the masters of the therapeutic arts"—those who are purported by their colleagues and their clients to have an intuitive and an exceptional grasp of meaningful ways of struggling with resistive patterns in therapeutic relationships.

I plan to take a year's sabbatical leave from my teaching and clinical practice and to visit with therapists who are regarded as exceptionally efficacious in their work with various kinds of therapeutic resistance and dilemmas. I plan to observe, experience, and question both the practitioners and their clients. I will develop a focused dialogue interview in which I will seek to experientially respond to each of these practitioners' ability to influence those with whom they are involved, as I struggle to both appreciate and to understand the practitioner's sentiments and ideas as they emerge in his therapeutic work. This is to say, I will try to understand the practitioner's impact with those whom I am interviewing, by letting my own resistance to how he or she may work emerge freely as I am encountering the practitioner. I will seek to come to appreciate their skills, alleged or real, by how I experience their dealing with my own personal refractory stances in dealing with my being-together with them. In short, I plan to investigate therapeutic artistry experientially from my own subjective involvement as a participant in these endeavors.

I will tape-record these dialogues in order to pull together the values, basic motifs, and central forces in the work and the influence of these masters of the therapeutic arts. I will, in turn, tape my own reactions to these tapes and send them back to the practitioner for his or her rejoinder, so that a dialogue can be maintained between us. In sorting out the motifs and processes from these dialogues, I will be most interested in how these practitioners deal with the crucial ethical (existential) concerns that I have raised in my book, *Therapeutic Partnership* (1977[a]), such as: "How far do we go in trying to help others?" and "How do we go about trying to answer this concern for ourselves as practitioners and enable our clients to answer it for themselves?"

These are the grounds for my pilot study. I hope, after a period of preliminary investigation, to set up more rigorous studies, testing hypotheses for this investigation in terms of (1) focus in psychotherapy; (2) questionnaires to make prediction; (3) criteria to evaluate programs for training of psychotherapists; and (4) investigate the issues indispensable for establishing psychotherapeutic contracts (see Goldberg, 1977[a]).

Having formulated some firm notions as to how the struggle between therapist and client imposes ethical and epistemological dilemmas in psychotherapy and how these concerns may be meaningfully addressed, I will seek ways of utilizing these processes in the training and education of both beginning and more experienced psychotherapists with whom I will be personally involved and those to whom I will be directing my future writing.

How will I choose which therapsits to investigate? I will set up a survey questionnaire that will enable me to assess whom other therapists regard as masters of the therapeutic arts, and a related issue.[1]

The questionnaire I plan to utilize reads as follows:

"Questionnaire Concerning Master Therapists"

"If you could choose any supervisor or consultant for your psychotherapy work, who would you choose? List ten practitioners in order of preference. Please indicate on the following sheets of this questionnaire why you have selected these particular persons. Your reply may be as lengthy as you like. These persons may be alive or deceased. They may be persons you have met, have had direct experience with, or only know by reputation, or by reading their work. Please make a second list of ten persons you would work with as your own therapist. The same conditions pertain as to the first list. To the extent that this list and the first list differ, please indicate why a person is on one list and not on the other. For both lists please indicate, to the best of your knowledge, where these persons currently reside. Finally, please make a third list of ten persons or characters who are fictional or legendary or persons who lived before the age of psychotherapy who, you believe, would have made excellent therapists or supervisors and explain why.

To summarize, make *three* lists:
1. Ten persons you would prefer as supervisor.
2. Ten persons you would prefer as therapists.
3. Ten persons you believe would have made excellent therapists or supervisors that lived prior to the age of psychotherapy or existed only in legend or fiction.

Please give explanations for including these persons on your lists!"

Postnote

Mental health practice has not reached the maturity of a science. Before this can occur, practitioners must carefully address several important ethical and epistemological issues (Goldberg, 1978). My investigation is an attempt to scrutinize these concerns in the work and practice of the masters of the therapeutic arts.

Psychotherapy, like all other interpersonal relationships, consists of a host of complex and interacting dimensions and parameters, certain of which stand out in importance. In order to develop more fully the therapeutic encounter as a meaningful human endeavor, practitioners need to know how these factors interact and to appreciate more clearly the particular shape these parameters take in a wide range of different psychotherapy and clinical situations. I will not try to maintain that I or anyone else knows for certain what all these factors are, but I will insist that practitioners know more than critics of psychotherapy generally claim. I also feel that practitioners have not been as straightforward and steadfast in looking at the crucial philosophical issues behind the more apparent clinical problems. My approach in investigating masters of the therapeutic arts, while admittedly subject to numerous potential errors of inclusion and exclusion, some ignorance, some presuppositions, and a bit of hope and apprehension, will, I believe, help systematize what practitioners do know about psychotherapy—helping to posit the essential factors to be considered in evaluating psychotherapy, and perhaps most important in the long run, helping to postulate a set of hypotheses to be tested empirically.

The approach I will be utilizing in my investigation explores psychotherapy and other clinical situations as an interpersonal dialogue in which certain conditions, in particular interactions, occur. Successful psychotherapy, from this orientation, results from the sufficient articulation of these interpersonal dimensions. Curiously, the research literature, as I read it, does not emphasize interpersonal conditions in psychotherapy, but focuses instead on what appears to be a sum total of desirable therapist and client personal attributes. This appears to lead to the notion that successful therapy results from the proper client-therapist matching. Moreover, whereas the personal trait model may be useful in the selection of therapists-to-be-trainted (because of supposed probability of "success"), such an approach does little or nothing to help the already practicing psychotherapist. This model merely points to personal traits the practitioner either has or does not have. It does not help him become aware of the important conditions that must be fostered and issues that must be struggled with in psychotherapy. In short, personal warmth, congruence, genuineness, accurate empathy, and unconditional positive regard may be essential personal traits of the effective therapist (as several investigators have demonstrated), but it is not simply because some therapists possess these traits that they are conducive to successful treatment. These personal traits are important only to the extent that they are useful in fostering certain crucial conditions in a therapeutic relationship. It is these crucial conditions that I propose to investigate in the quest for meaning in the psychotherapy encounter with the therapeutic masters.

The kind of investigation I am proposing, to my knowledge, is unique. The few attempts to investigate the "quality" of therapists' work have been either transcripts of their sessions with patients or journalistic and innane interviews with the practitioner, such as Adelaide Bry's *Inside Psychotherpay* (Basic Books, 1972). An exception to this pattern was Jane Howard's *Please Touch* (McGraw-Hill, 1970). Howard, during the height of the sensitivity training movement, visited and participated in a dozen or so different kinds of encounter groups and other sensitivity modality experiences. But while her report was a lucid description of the sociological conditions surrounding these groups and personal descriptions of the encounter leaders, her absence of expertise as a psychotherapist prevented her from successfully penetrating into the practitioners' work and delineating their art in an epistemologically meaningful way.

It seems to me that a preferred place to start an investigation of epistemological concerns in psychotherapy is to purview therapeutic situations in which the work is caught up in therapeutic impasse, or where either or both of the therapeutic agents experiences himself or the other agent resisting the therapeutic work for which they have convened. It is my contention that crucial ethical issues (Goldberg, 1977[a]) are being broached in these clinical situations. My research and my clinical experience as a practitioner and a psychotherapy educator have made it abundantly clear as I have argued in the last chapter that the fulcrum of all therapeutic endeavor resides in the struggle between therapist and client as to how meaningfully each will permit himself and the other agent to become involved in the therapeutic relationship. It seems to me that "failures" (the lack of reduction of symptoms) can be useful and significant to therapeutic work if this struggle between therapist and client can be consciously related to the establishment of meaning; that is to say, utilizing therapeutic resistance to promote efficacious ways of being-in-the-world. Yet, as I indicated in the last chapter, this therapeutic struggle is not central to major theories of psychotherapy. These psychological theories, as a result, fail to consider therapeutic resistance as a product of the failure to adequately address crucial ethical conserns evoked by the ways both therapist and client come together to create meaning for their being-in-the-world.

Conclusion

"For an artist true-born revolt is second nature: he is both tribune and trouble-maker."

—A. Vozhesensky

   This volume has been a series of essays on modern man—that which he is—with some attempt to account for how he became that way and why he has chosen to remain as he is.

   We have pursued these existential concerns in terms of the psychology of the creative Self. The psychology of the creative Self, as I have argued, begins with the nature of intentionality. To be born is to be thrust into being-in-the-world. The intention of human existence is experienced in the progressive trend by the Self toward embracing its being-in-the-world in reaching out to touch, encounter, and merge with objects of its expanding consciousness. It is an urge to revel in being-in-the-world. But at every dimension of its existence, at every moment of its course in the world, there are forces, both internal and beyond itself, that oppose and thwart its active being. These are the myriad powers that deny the Self's purposive existence and its paths to expanded consciousness. These are the forces that endeavor to lead the Self to deny and diminish itself. These forces may appear irresistible. Albeit, the instant that the Self gives in to these forces it has questioned its validity as an intending being. From that moment—whether the final moment is a matter of moments, days, or even decades—the fate of the Self is sealed, the Self is doomed to the stolid confines of its own embarrassment and dissuasion. The Self in this stance has disinherited itself and accepted the verdict of banishment from its full being-in-the-world. Obviously, as mortals, as finite beings, we are all victims of this ontological dissuasion. Fortunately, the Self can temper its dissuasion by its creative struggle to find meaning for itself.

In the passage below I will briefly summarize how the self mitigates against its creative struggles, leading to its ontological malaise.

The difficulty modern man has had in trying to find out how he intends his being-in-the-world is derived from his assumption that his sentiments reside in his "inner Self"—somehow to be revealed by introspection and or psychotherapy. In this volume I have offered an alternative perspective on modern man: We come to know who we are and how we intend our presence-in-the-world in terms of our actions. Our feelings and our intentions are lucid and meaningful in terms of our interactions with other Selves and in our commitments to projects in the world, rather than in inferred and hypothetical abstraction of what we might really be. We experience the quality of our being in terms of our decisions and actions, in our preferences and the meaning we ascribe to our own behavior, as well as to that of how others treat us.

The Self is drawn to propitious moments. There come times for each Self when the Self must choose or forever lose the name of action. We need to realize that our difficulty with action resides not in our endeavor to find solutions to our problems and concerns, but rather, that we seek to find problems for which we have already formulated answers. Each of us has accrued a great deal of information and enlightened experience; moreover, each of us at various choice points in our lives has made some kind of semi-aware decision about how to process these experiences and what to do about them in terms of the person we intend to be. Our obsessions over our decisions are indicative of our own disrespect and self-denigration with our intuitive being. Moreover, no matter how well obsessively derived decisions turn out *prima facie,* in the meantime other decisions could not be made—as each decision and action (as I have argued in chapters four and five) enables us to further liberate ourselves. The Self takes action, therefore, not only on a particular course of concern, but no less importantly, to free itself to make other decisions.

I invalidate my trepidation and confirm my courage when I realize that I could have done nothing other than I did in the past, because I could not be someone other than who I was. Having experienced the past, I can utilize these experiences to realize choice for myself. And in taking action on these choices, I become who I am. In choosing, we confirm our presence, giving ourselves and the world in which we find ourselves a reality. Not, perhaps, the best of all possible worlds! But we have no choice about the world in which we have been thrust. The choice we do have is what we do—how creatively and meaningfully we deal—with what we are confronted. If we remain passive and so attempt to deny and ignore having been thrust into a less than perfect world, we are acted upon and dissuaded from the reality of our own ontological presence. This gradual process may continue until we go out of existence.

I have come to realize that the psychotherapy clients I have seen through the years have chosen to deny their existence. I now realize that the boredom I experienced in being a practitioner derived from encountering and allowing myself to bear my time with shadows of men and women. To a considerable extent they have chosen not to exist for themselves, for me, or for anyone else. Their complaints have been repetitious. I've heard the same "stories" over and over again. I often wondered if these stories were the only ones they allowed themselves to relate. They have given themselves, as I have for myself, plausible explanations (excuses) for their not being fully-in-the-world. To the extent that they or I excuse ourselves, we dissuade ourselves of the contents of our consciousness; to that extent we do not exist.

In summary, the Self is not a fixed entity at any moment in time—which need lose or give up its integrity (What it "is")—but rather the Self is a potential, a pro-active striving to become what it seeks to be—to become authentic to its intentionality. The reality of the Self, therefore, is not a conservatiion of what it has been heretofore but what it seeks to be. To be conservative of what the Self has been is the surrender of the Self to non-being. To become passionate about its emergence is for the Self to become alive. The creative Self attempts to enjoy its experiences as it is experienced by the Self, regardless of the "real motive" of the Self and others involved.

NOTES

Chapter One – The Ethical Requirements of a Self Theory

[1]Maddi (1967) in a thoughtful article has differentiated existential alienation from that of neurosis. The meaninglessness experienced in existential alienation is characterized by Maddi as

> the chronic inability to believe in the truth, importance, usefulness, or interest value of any of the things one is engaged in or can imagine doing. The most characteristic features of the affective tone are blandness and boredom, punctuated by periods of depression...activity level may be low to moderate, but more [importantly these] activities are not chosen. There is little selectivity, it being immaterial to the person what if any activities he pursues. If there is any selectivity shown, it is in the direction of ensuring minimal expenditure of effort and decision-making.

[2]Consensus reality is an encounter in which each Self reveals itself as it intends to be and is responded to as the Self is experienced by others in projecting itself-in-the-world. The basis for exchanges is determined by negotiation rather than by external systems of equity (see Goldberg, 1977[a] and Appendix D of this volume).

[3]My formal training in philosophy was as an undergraduate philosophy major.

[4]Parenthetically, although Sigmund Freud was himself a classical scholar and most probably aware of the meaning of *aréte* (courage in the face of inevitable fate), as suggested in his definition of psychotherapy as changing that which can be changed and to accept that which cannot be changed, this noble ancient concept and its implications seems to have been largely lost in modern psychotherapy; although Victor Frankl (1964) illustrated the concept in his very moving account of his own experiences in the concentration camps of World War II.

Chapter Two – The Saga of Don Juan Retold

[1]Percy Shelley *Adonais.*

[2]Ibid.

[3]*El Burlador de Sevilla.*

[4]Winter (1975) reports that Otto Rank's thesis on Don Juan is the only extended psychological interpretation of the legend of any substance. Other psychological studies of the theme include Marañon (1940), Worthington (1962), Pratt (1960), Winter (1963), and Weinstein (1959). Among the psychoanalysts, Reik (1945), and Fenichel (1945) refer briefly to Don Juan. Curiously, Winter indicates, he was not able to locate any reference to Don Juan in any of Freud's works, although Schur (1972) has mentioned Freud's keen fondness for Mozart's *Don Giovanni.*

[5]This act was called by Shaw "Don Juan in Hell."

[6]Rank (Winter, 1975) helps us realize why Don Juan's trepidation fails to be noticed by casual observation. Rank writes: " . . . it would be impossible to create the Don Juan figure, the frivolous Knight without conscience and without fear of death or the devil, if a part of that

Don Juan were not thereby split off in Leporello [Don Juan's servant and his helper in his clever schemes], who represents the inner criticism, the anxiety, and the conscience of the hero" (p. 51).

[7]Thus, Don Juan slays God, as we shall see later in this chapter, by rejecting him, and in the legend he actually slays the commandant (Donna Anna's father) in a duel. Don Juan cannot tolerate any arbitrary, vain, or unreasonable authority that stands in his way. Only reason assuages Juan.

[8]W. H. Auden. "September 1, 1939." In Auden, W. H., *The English Auden*. Random House, New York, 1977, pp. 245–246.

[9]A concept to be explained later in this chapter.

[10]In *Six Characters in Search of an Author*.

[11]George Gordon (Lord Byron). *Don Juan*.

[12]Ovid. *Metamorphoses*.

[13]The need to justify his existence may well be a thinly disguised struggle of Don Juan with parricidic guilt. In Rank's thesis (Winter, 1975) on the Don Juan legend, he demonstrates a progression of presumed cultural evolution " . . . in which the belief that death is caused by the hostile wishes of a living person leads to guilt about these hostile wishes due to the fear that the dead will return to avenge their 'murderer' " (p. 21).

[14]This is still another feature that informs Don Juan as a modern protagonist.

[15]It is important to note that although efforts are being made here to differentiate philosophical depression from other affective moods, in reality, philosophical depression may change to, merge with, or be co-existent with other forms of depression.

[16]Ovid. *Metamorphoses*.

Chapter Five—A Theory of Emotions—Emotionality as the Expression of the Self's Intentionality

[1]I am particularly concerned in this chapter with those behavioral sciences that deal directly with human suffering—such as clinical psychology and psychiatry.

[2]In this Chapter I am less interested in differentiating and categorizing human emotions as in evincing emotionality as a vital human activity that reveals the Self's concerns in constituting itself-in-the-world.

[4]The development of human meaning is such a complex process that I cannot hope to delineate its evolution in a step-by-step manner as in, let us say, describing the building of a material edifice. Rather, I will be discussing issues, concerns, and developmental requirements as these factors interact and interface with each other.

Chapter Six—Twilight of the Gods

[1]The character of the Father in *Six Characters in Search of an Author*.

[2]This, quite naturally, contributes to the narcissistic feeling that there is so much to me that whatever is glimmered of me is only a fraction of my vast and variegated Self and, hence, is misleading.

[3]I have found in reflecting that as a writer I was far more productive, actually spending more time writing, in the past when I had the heaviest schedule working full-time as a therapist or a director of a community mental health center, teaching, and consulting, together with a part-time, private practice.

I now realize that I used writing to escape and buffer myself against others. Now, having more time to write, I find other distractions to keep me from the onerous task of writing. But, perhaps, more fairly to myself, the work I do now is more to deal directly with myself rather than externalize my self-doubts through objective and intellectual pursuits.

Chapter Seven—The Paradoxical Journey in Search of Self

[1]Barney is an acquaintance, not a psychotherapy client.

Chapter Eight—Paradoxical Approaches in Psychotherapy

[1]To understand my rationale for the "absurdity" I was conveying to the family, the reader needs to substitute the concept "responsibility" for the word "worrying."

[2]C. Whitaker (1978) has indicated that one of the major values of the paradoxical approach is that it enables the client to seriously consider whether the therapist is crazier than he, the patient. However, in doing so, he, the patient, must seriously take into consideration his own craziness and its ramifications.

[3]In a book I am now preparing, I explore in considerable detail some single cases.

[4]The Cocktail Party.

Chapter Nine—Creating Meaning in Psychotherapy

[1]These critics fail to recognize the rather obvious lawfulness the development of will requires—a lawfulness that perhaps does not accord with scientific determinism, but why must it!

[1]This is similar to the social-worker client described in chapter eight.

Chapter Ten—An Investigation of Masters of the Therapeutic Arts

[1]I am curious about a phenomenon in the reputation of therapists which I refer to as the "Myth of the Favorite Son" (See Appendix B).

Appendix C

[1]A detailed description of these existential situations and their rationale is found in Goldberg, 1977[a]; Chapter Six.

Appendix D

1This section is an updated version of material found on pages 138–142 of a previous book (Goldberg, 1977[a]).

[2]There are two classes of selfishness. Destructive selfishness rewards weakness and failure. The person who is overweight and claims he wishes to diet may, for example, reward (console) himself for the emptiness of his life by consuming rich foods. He, in short, eats to celebrate the inability to feel good about himself. Constructive selfishness rewards (celebrates) work and success. The person with an alcohol problem, for example, no longer has a drinking problem when he only celebrates accomplishments that make him feel good about himself. In short, he celebrates his ability to feel good about himself.

[3]Power adequacy I have defined previously as the inner experience of being aware of one's personel needs; knowing that the resources to satisfy them are available; and realizing that to utilize one's power, one needs the ability and persmission to obtain these resources. (See Goldberg, 1977[a], pp. 95–97, for the relationship of power adequacy to psychotherapy.)

Appendices

"Curse on all laws but those which love has made."

—Anonymous

Appendix A

"The utilization of a proverb inventory to examine belief systems."

This project is an example of what James Miller (1969) once proposed as "giving away psychology"—changing people through education—teaching them to use psychological, educational, and psychotherapeutic concepts to give meaning to their lives. Some experienced practitioners regard educational endeavors to improve psychological functioning as "psychologizing" —that is to say, merely an intellectual exercise without any meaningful emotional realization. As a result, they have left the promising endeavor of "change" through education to poorly trained and exploitative practitioners to take advantage of a ravenous demand for psychological education among the populace.

In my work as a director of a community mental health center, I became deeply impressed by the many different kinds of strength, resource, and comfort people in a community offer to one another. Each of us is, no doubt, aware of the old folk remedies for colds, warts, and for various pains and ailments that have been passed down from one generation to the next, from one neighbor to another. We may be less aware of old folk remedies for offering sympathy and condolence, as well as support and encouragement of those who are bogged down and depressed by life's vicissitudes. These remedies, too, have been passed down by one generation to the next in the form of various folk tales, adages, and proverbs. The use of proverbs as an ethical and common-sense guide for living is perhaps as ancient as man's earliest awakenings of social thought. Proverbs represent, by employment of generalizations, a vivid and immediate description of the conditions in which common man finds himself. In condensed statement, proverbs convey to other men strategies and attitudes that may be adapted in face of these conditions to render life more gratifying, ordered, and understandable. For example, the proverb "Large oaks from little acorns grow" may be interpreted to mean that large ventures may have small beginnings. It may also suggest that patience has its reward.

I wrote a weekly newspaper column on mental health while director of a community mental health center. I seriously considered writing on the wisdom contained in proverbs and discussing how a person's reaction to proverbs may tell us much about the attitudes each of us has toward life and how these attitudes influence our happiness, productivity, and relationship with family, friends and acquaintances. I considered providing an inventory in the first installment of the article on proverbs and giving explanations for the patterns of replies by the readers in the second installment Because I left the center soon after toying with this project, I never did submit it to the newspaper. I still do believe that the concept has considerable merit, and because it is an illustration of the principles I have been discussing in this volume, I will delineate the inventory here.

I described proverbs in the proposed articles (similar to what I have already discussed) and then went on to indicate:

> "First, it should be pointed out that for each proverb generalizing about the desirability of a certain course of action, it is generally possible to find another course of action under similar circumstances. This would suggest that no proverb expresses an absolutely correct or workable solution to a problematic situation. People may be expected therefore to differ in interpreting and agreeing with the desirability of an action and the action conveyed in any proverb. However, consideration of the reasons people employ for agreement or disagreement with a series of proverbs may be helpful to that person in understanding his own attitudes toward life and other people."

I have listed below a series of ten familiar proverbs. Under each proverb I have given four possible reasons for agreeing *or* disagreeing with the message contained in the proverb. For each of the ten proverbs first *circle* the alternative (a, b, c, or d) which is the *closest to your own point of view*. It is, of course, possible that none of the alternatives (a, b, c, or d) will be in complete agreement with your own point of view for some or all of the proverbs. Nonetheless, please indicate the alternative which is *closest* to your point of view. Also, it is possible that you agree with more than one alternative, but please only indicate *one* alternative for each proverb.

1. *"A stream cannot rise higher than its source."*

    a. *Agree* because people are limited by heredity and past experience.

    b. *Disagree* because we can accomplish as much as we are willing to strive for.

    c. *Disagree* because while effort goes a long way, a person needs to get enough encouragement along the way.

    d. *Neither* because success is being at the right place at the right time.

2. *Where there is a will there is a way."*

    a. *Agree* because things are possible through work and effort.

    b. *Disagree* because there are things in this world which no one can change.

    c. *Agree* because a belief in God, one's self, or one's fellow man can move mountains.

    d. *Disagree* because luck and opportunity play an important role in life and to a large degree determine how much one can really accomplish.

3. *"Strike while the iron is hot."*

    a. *Disagree* because if something is meant to be, it will happen regardless of what a person does.

    b. *Agree* because we must forge ahead whenever we can as long as no one's fingers get burned in the process.

    c. *Agree* because if we don't take advantage of our opportunities, it is no one's fault but ours.

    d. *Neither* because chance tells us where to stand .

4. *"It is better to light one small candle than forever curse the darkness."*

    a. *Agree* because a person doesn't have the right to expect more in life than his share.

b. *Disagree* because it is beyond the power of any individual to change what is meant to be.

c. *Disagree* because a person doesn't have the right to be satisfied unless everyone can share in the good things in life.

d. *Disagree* because a person has a right to achieve his ambitions and a right to eliminate obstacles that block his way.

5. *"Discretion is the better part of valor."*

a. *Neither* because one's destiny once begun cannot be rerouted.

b. *Agree* because a man is responsible first to himself.

c. *Disagree* because a man must do his duty—his own feelings and judgment have little to do with it.

d. *Agree* because if we were meant to be brave we would have been constituted that way.

6. *"The sun shines upon all alike."*

a. *Agree* because no man has any more right to the good things in life than any other man.

b. *Disagree* because some people burn and others tan—that is just the way people are born.

c. *Disagree* because some people have advantages of background and education.

d. *Disagree* because a man's place in the sun is determined by his own efforts.

7. *"A disease known is half cured."*

a. *Disagree* because why brood about something you can't do anything about?

b. *Disagree* because what is must be accepted.

c. *Agree* because often what we regard as disease is fear and ignorance, and they can be overcome.

d. *Agree* because illness is an inability to reach and be reached by others.

8. *"Never have poor workmen good tools."*

a. *Agree* because desire and commitment are the most formidable of tools.

b. *Agree* because ability is a gift.

c. *Disagree* because a man is entitled to be resentful of his lack of opportunity and natural ability.

d. *Agree* because a man who works for others' welfare should never complain about his working conditions.

9. *"Man proposes but God disposes."*

a. *Agree* because man's free will is an illusion.

b. *Agree* because what will be will be!

c. *Agree* because there are universal laws that govern a man's behavior that go beyond his individual wants.

d. *Disagree* because a man can either choose the rules he lives by or permit others to choose rules for him.

10. *"He travels swiftest who travels alone."*

a. *Neither* because accomplishments are empty if they do not contribute to another's happiness.

b. *Agree* because if a person wants something done, it is he who must do it.

c. *Disagree* because no one can foresee what obstacles lie in his path.

d. *Agree* because sometimes two people are just poison for each other.

How to Score and Evaluate the Reader's Responses to the Proverb Inventory:

The proverbs contained in last week's column may be helpful to the reader in assessing his own point of view in regard to the responsibility he assumes toward the conditions of his life situation. To score one's responses to these proverbs, do the following on a blank sheet of paper:

Write on the top of the sheet the words: "Fate", "Social Responsibility", and "Personal Responsibility." Under "Fate" give yourself *one point each* for having circled each of the following alternatives:

Question 1 A or D

" 2 . B or D

"	3	A or D
"	4	A or B
"	5	A or D
"	6	B or C
"	7	A or B
"	8	B or C
"	9	A or B
"	10	C or D

For "Social Responsibility" give yourself *one point each* for having circled each of the following alternatives:

Question 1		C
"	2	C
"	3	B
"	4	C
"	5	C
"	6	A
"	7	D
"	8	D
"	9	C
"	10	A

For "Personal Responsibility" give yourself *one point each* for having circled each of the following alternatives:

Quesion 1		B
"	2	A
"	3	C
"	4	D
"	5	B
"	6	D
"	7	C
"	8	A
"	9	D
"	10	B

What Do the Scores Mean?

A score of four or more suggests a tendency to adopt one of the three points of three contained in attitude and, possibly, in action. For example, a person with a score of four or more on "Personal Responsibility" is a person who feels that it is incumbent upon him to strive for those things he seeks. He relies a great deal on his own resources and counsel and may forge ahead even if others disapprove of his efforts. A person with a score of four or more on "Social Responsibility" is a person who relies a great deal on the counsel and support of others and is often hesitant to forge ahead if others disapprove of his efforts. A person with a score of four or more on "Fate" is a person who feels that his own efforts are not greatly effective, that most of the important things are beyond his power to change or determine. He may take a stoic philosophical attitude toward life and accept events with resignation or at times become upset and frustrated at his inability to take control over the conditions influencing his life.

A combination of any of the three points of view are possible in this inventory.

How the Inventory Can be Helpful to the Reader

This inventory is not intended to label a person as being a certain type or possessing a certain kind of psychological problem. To the contrary, we suggest that the interested reader check out the kind of point of view he received on this inventory with his friends and family members to see how they perceive his outlook on life. This, hopefully, will evoke a lively and rich discussion of how each of the persons involved is affected by the reader's philosophical attitudes and how in turn they respond to him.

Appendix B

The Myth of the Favorite Son

Local pride is a quality of life we generally take for granted. The Californian is proud of his vineyards. He argues the virtues of California wines with as much ego-involvement as the French or Spanish *aficionado*. The native New Yorker still thinks New York City is the greatest place on earth to live. He is puzzled by the attraction of San Francisco for some people, where people still use old-fashioned trolley cars, and Paris, where horsemeat is a delicacy. Each locale is equally proud of its native sons. Plaques and monuments are erected by proud neighbors to indicate where famous natives were born or bred. It is an almost far-gone assumption that despite the opponent's political strength throughout the nation, infrequently does he carry native son's home state, rarely the opponent's home community. Political conventions are marked by long-winded speeches by delegates for their favorite sons.

If this phenomenon is a deeply ingrained feature of American life, it may be expected that it touches every segment of American life, including the sector of the profession of psychotherapy.

A number of observations have caused me to requestion the notion of the favorite son in terms of attitudes and beliefs among professional psychotherapists. A number of personal experiences are pertinent here. Several years ago I wrote a book that sold rather well. I frequently met people from other parts of the nation and abroad who had read the book or after meeting them at conventions or elsewhere were interested in reading my book. On the other hand, few of even my closest friends, including professional colleagues, have read the book or seem very eager to do so. Other professional colleagues who have written books have reported similar reactions. Moreover, whereas I have consulted and given workshops in my own home area, it is far more frequent that I receive the best consulting and workshop offers from other parts of the country. Other colleagues, again, have mentioned similar experiences. One cogently expressed the myth of the favorite son in the following formula:

> If you live in the same city as the requesting agency you are seen as doing work in your specialty. If you have to travel a 100-mile distance or more for that consultation, you are regarded as knowledgable in the field. If you travel 500 miles or more you are regarded as an expert.

And, finally, I observed several years ago, after leaving a mental health department to go into full-time practice, that the same professional colleagues were willing to pay me for supervision when I was in private practice who weren't interested in my supervision for *gratis* when I worked in the same agency as they.

Appendix C

Existential Dilemma Inventory

Instructions: This inventory is intended to help you get in touch with your own core values as they interface your existential concerns. The situations you will be asked to respond to may initially appear far-fetched. You should be able to derive some meaning from them if you regard these situations as *immediate* and *real.*

Each situation in this inventory should be read and answered in succession. Do not turn to the next situation before answering preceding questions.

1. Lifeboat Situation.

In keeping with the notion that only the present is immediate and real, I would like you, as best you can, to consider as immediate and real the following situation: You are in a lifeboat in the middle of the Atlantic Ocean far off from shore and without any real hope for immediate rescue. There are six other people in the boat.

A. Who are these people? (They should be people whom you have met or know personally. You may name as many or as few of these people as you like.)

1.	4.
2.	5.
3.	6.

You find the boat is springing water. There is too much weight in the boat. Someone has to be dropped overboard to save the others, or the whole boat with everyone will go down. (This is the given task. Please do not try to find intellectual means to avert the task, as this will invalidate the value of the inventory.)

B. Who will go overboard?

C. How would it be that this person would go overboard?

D. How do you feel about this?

E. How are you involved in this person going overboard?

It now appears that only *one* person in the lifeboat can be saved.

F. Who will this person be?

G. How will it be decided and why?

H. How do you feel about this?

I How are you involved?

2. Epitaph Exercise.

I would like you to sum up the essence of your life. This is more frequently done by others. It is usually someone else who writes an epitaph for one whose existence has terminated. I would like you to make a terse statement or two in which you summarize your life, as if your existence were now terminated.

3. The Except For! Exercise.

I would like you to get in touch with what has been and is still missing in your existence. You can do this in the following form: I would have *done* _____, I would have *felt* _____, I would have *cared* _____, except for _____!

4. The Potlatch Exercise.

I would like you to think about your personality and to select that aspect of yourself—that trait or attribute—that you like and/or other people admire most about you, and then symbolically discard that attribute; that is, "disown" that trait for the purposes of the exercise. Then I would like you to describe how you feel about yourself, now that you have cast away what you regard as a vital component of your personal functioning.

5. Discussion of exercises.[1]

A. Were you able to get into the situations and experience them as immediate and real?
B. What were the situations like for you?
C. How did you experience yourself?
D. What did you learn about yourself?
E. What values and meaning emanated from these exercises?

Appendix D

Basic Emotional Communication[1]

If practitioners are concerned about the plight of the individuals in distress with whom they work, they must first uncover the issues that predicate the individual's place in the social order. Emotional disturbance, as I argued in a previous book (Goldberg, 1977[a]), is a result of deterioration and disequilibrium of equity and balance that an individual experiences in relationship to significant others in his normative system. If equity and balance are essential interpersonal dimensions for maximizing one's place in society, the client must be taught how to negotiate directly for restoration of these relations in his interpersonal and societal transactions. To seek out the reasons why the client has feared to ask for equity in his object relations is not sufficient. For the client to become a more responsible and effective person, he needs to be given responsibility for collaborating in his own emotional growth. This endeavor requires a partnership between therapist and client.

I have argued (Goldberg, 1977[a]) that all transactions between people are contractual. The therapeutic relationship I have proposed differs from that of other interpersonal situations in that the contractual obligations of the agents involved in a therapeutic encounter are or should be based upon a voluntary, intentional, informed, and goal-directed agreement as to how each will conduct himself with the other. By focusing upon the transactional and contractual dimensions within the therapeutic relationship, the therapist has the opportunity to become aware of the effect his own values and sentiments have upon shaping the client's behavior in ways the client may or may not intend. To foster a relationship in which the client can learn to contract for his wants in an effective and responsible manner, the therapeutic partnership needs to be viewed as an autonomous system. Neither therapist nor client can be beholden to any third party in their dealings with one another. Where the practitioner is a double agent—representing the state or a school of psychotherapy and its dogma or being reimbursed by a third party—there is serious intrusion upon the partnership relationship. In my therapeutic model, the client is not relegated to the role of victim of his inscrutable nature and circumstance and in need of being taken care of by the therapist. The therapist's function is not to change the client but to help him discover his intentionality so that he may have more conscious choices about how he lives his existence. My model supports the theoretical positions of Szasz, Haley, and others who hold that conventional psychotherapy based upon a medical model, whether conducted by physicians or nonmedical practitioners, creates an implicit status relationship that serves to exacerbate the client's denigratory sense of self. The model I have proposed requires speaking and dealing personally with clients. For too long, Schaffer (1974) argues, practitioners "have been content automatically to use a fundamentally impersonal diction: it seems so safe and effective, so tried-and-true. But working only in that way no longer seems adequate to the variety of situations we encourage or arrange."

Psychotherapy as a contractual partnership offers the client a fair, reasonable and efficacious treatment modality. It may not always be a welcome prospect for the client, however. Unlike the traditional medical model, in which the client places a blind trust in the practitioner's knowledge and healing powers, contractual psychotherapy replaces magic with hard work.

The client may initially feel it is unfair to assume collaborative responsibilities when he is feeling confused, exhausted, and distressed. Because he experiences himself as inadequate, he willingly pays a therapist to resolve his difficulties. Only from the practitioner's willingness to share his own humanity with the client does the client come to the realization that he cannot escape his ontological responsibilities if he is to find meaning in his existence.

In the following pages I discuss a special kind of dialogue which I have labelled "Basic Emotional Communication". I am proposing the utilization of basic emotional communication for the following two purposes in this book:

Firstly, as a means for persons involved in intimate and significant relations to explore their relationship; secondly, as a model for resolving conflict and moving beyond impasse in the therapist-client relationship. In my experience, equity and balance are maintained or reestablished when exchanges are based on the procedures of basic emotional communications.

Basic emotional communication (BEC) consists of a dialogue occurring between two or more individuals involved in a significant relationship in which the needs of each are both heard and resonded to, emotionally as well as cognitively. The aim of this task is to keep the momentum going in a realtionship. A useful analogy to the process of basic emotional communication would be to keep a pingpong ball in motion on a table through the continual strokes of each of the two players. Such an exchange requires that neither player try to move the ball out of the reach of the other in order to win a point; otherwise the ball would hit the floor and cease to be in motion.

BEC is built upon the guidelines of dialectical process and, as such, has a temporal structure. The partners

> alternate in their presentations, and each successive statement has to reflect at least the one immediately preceding. Incorporating only the preceding statements represents, of course, a minimum requirement for a dialogue. A maximum is attained if each utterance reflects all of the earlier statements. Strictly speaking, one never enters the same dialogue twice. Each utterance must be consistent with the [other's] own views and must represent equally consistent or systematically modified reactions to all statements made by the [other]. [Riegel, 1976]

Moreover, each alternating statement must reflect the same basic theme the speaker has presupposed and, until that moment, not consciously realized. If a reflective coordination is not built into the dialectical process:

> the dialogue would degenerate into alternating monologues in which each [partner] would merely follow up on his or her earlier statements without reacting to the [other's] elaborations. The [other's] statements would appear

as distractive interruptions and the only remaining dialogic feature would consist of the alternations between the [partners]. [Riegel, 1976]

BEC is still in the process of refinement. At present, it consists of the following twenty-three instructions based on the concepts of equity and balance and the existential principles presented throughout a previous volume (Goldberg, 1977[a]).

1. Speak directly and personally to the other.

Assume that the other Self has no previous information about you, that the other will know you entirely on the basis of what you are willing to reveal in this specific encounter.

2. Make "I" statements, rather than "you" statements.

Take ownership of your statements. This will move both partners away from blaming, dependent, object-fused stances and toward positive, direct statements of want and desire.

3. Make statements out of your questions.

This keeps the momentum going in a dialogue by moving the exchange away from excessive reflection, intellectualization, and, hence, hesitation.

4. Make statements of your present feelings rather than of your thoughts or previous feelings.

Interpersonal conflict, particularly in significant relationships, centers around the issue of arguing "facts" rather than stating preferences. Making statements of present feelings, therefore, moves the exchange onto an emotional experiential plane in which the wants and the desires of both partners are open to sharing, exploring, and negotiating, rather than one in which demands are presented as concluded (fixed) and closed (nonnegotiable). Emotions are facts not limited to any single means of expression. Using a constructively selfish approach,[2] ask directly for what you want and do not "protect" the other from "selfishness" (that is, your wants). Regard the other as capable of responsible and rational agreement or disagreement with your requests.

5. Make statements of your desired expectations rather than of what you hope to avoid.

This enables each of the partners to become aware of what is gratifying to the other Self rather than only of what the other wants to avoid. Psychologically, it is easier to initiate new behaviors than it is to terminate old ones. To do this, each of the partners must avoid apologizing for his feelings and his needs.

6. Specify exactly what is wanted.

It is important to be exact about what you are asking for in an exchange (for example, time and place) rather than simply to speak of wanting behaviors initiated or terminated. This is because, psychologically, an individual can best adjust his behaviors in a situation in which he knows specifically when these behaviors are most crucial to the other, as opposed to a situation in which he experiences himself as being expected completely to adapt or drop existing behaviors.

7. Keep your statements brief.

Clear and terse statements make it more convenient for the other to respond immediately. Elaborate and tangential statements are apt to cause the partner to lose the essence of the communicative intent.

8. Give feedback for clarity.

Periodically summarize (play back) what you have heard as objectively as you can. This provides a mirror for you to use to reflect upon what you are presenting to your partner.

9. When examining conflict in the relationship, avoid interpretations and value judgments.

Employing interpretations and value judgments effects an imbalance in the relationship by informing the partner that his behavior needs to be morally restructured according to your system of equity (Goldberg, 1977[a]) rather than according to explicitly negotiated norms established by both partners.

10. *Keep the momentum going in the exchange.*

A relationship feeds on the balance of energies contributed by the external system (that is, the two partners). You cannot, therefore, allow yourself to let the exchange abort by becoming upset or angry and tuning out.

11. *Use active terms in the exchange.*

We experience ourselves and others in the world in terms of the conceptualizations revealed in the language we employ. The use of active and dynamic terms and descriptions also helps to keep the momentum going in an exchange. The excessive use of passive terms reveals the passive use of Self and of its perception of itself as tentative-in-the-world. Passive conceptualization leads to the loss of momentum in the exchange.

12. *Move from a statement of needs to a statement of preference.*

Necessity and preference are often confused conceptually, as well as emotionally. Most people can meet their basic needs in order to survive, but they do not experience the "permission" (that is, power adequacy[3]) to want more than to meet these basic needs. Consequently, many people force themselves into positions of isolation, desperation, depression, and despair simply in order to secure some human contact. You don't have to need a response from your partner to ask for it.

13. *Be aware that your interpersonal involvement in a dialogue is dependent on your interpersonal risks.*

The cautious, introspective person becomes isolated and detached in an exchange, because he feels a need to express only statements of which he feels certain. This cautious stance erodes the dialogue until it loses its momentum. A basic emotional exchange is intended to be an opportunity for you to explore uncertain, uncomfortable, and threatening aspects of yourself with another person.

14. *Periodically attempt new modes of behavior with your partnership.*

It is particularly relevant "to do something different" when you feel threatened by your partner's not fulfilling your expectations of how you would like to be treated. To the extent that the Self maintains old modes of behavior, it is threatened by loss of its essence—its "real" Self (see chapters three, four, and five). To the extent that the Self periodically attempts new behaviors, it experiences energy and expansion of Self rather than a need to conserve its integrity against attack. For example, to say to oneself with feeling, "How interesting! I am curious about what is going to happen to me!" can be experienced with marked physiological, no less, than attitudinal changes.

15. Say "no" but never say "never"!

View the dialogue as an experiential laboratory for searching for a greater awareness of yourself and your partner, rather than as a situation in which personal limitations are to be judged. Let your partner know where you are at the moment, but leave the possibility of modification open for the future.

16. View strong feelings in an exchange as mediators of intentionality.

If in an exchange you feel bored, misunderstood, or unloved, you are required to act. Interpret states of feeling not as calls to remain passive and deprived, but as calls on you to enact the state of being you feel is lacking.

17. Act with the other as if the other partner is the person with whom you would like to be involved and as if you are the person you intend yourself to be.

I view personality, as I have reiterated throughout this volume, as a process rather than a fixed entity. A person becomes what he seeks to be through action and intent, rather than through passive induction of intrapsychic arousal and stimulation. A person is shaped toward being the kind of person another seeks him to be when he is treated as if he were that person. A person's intent, therefore, serves to role-model desired attributes he seeks in another.

18. When you experience unfulfilled gratification from your partner, initiate the gratifying behavior toward your partner.

If you feel unloved, it is likely that you are treating yourself as unlovable. Acting as if you are lovable, you are lovable. In an exchange, partners often become hung up on justification of their behavior by expecting and demanding reciprocal behaviors by their partner. One acts lovable toward another not only to evoke desired responses from the other, but to evoke desired responses in one's self.

19. Realize that you and your partner are not responsible in the dialogue to any outside agent.

In dysfunctional relationships, each of the agents attempts to manipulate the other into assuming his own idiosyncratic system of equity in exchanges. More functional dialogues result from realizing that neither partner is responsible to any outside agent or system of conduct in his interactions with the other.

20. Explicitly review norms, standards of conduct and other values brought in from society-at-large in preparation for negotiating them within the relationship.

Because you view your partner's contributions to the dialogue in the context of these values and sentiments, you need to decide how they function within this particular relationship, which because it represents a contractual arrangement between just the two of you, is open to renegotiation to improve functioning.

21. Avoid giving or asking for declarations of essence.

Many of the depressed and passive-resistant clients I have seen in psychotherapy are caught up in the tragically "romantic" trap of saying, "I don't really care how he (or she) treats me, as long as he (or she) says 'I love you'" and "I don't care whether the relationship ends or not as long as I feel that he (or she) loved me"! Love, or any other emotional condition, is not a single entity; it is a series of specific ways of relating to another person. The individual who refuses to ask directly for equitable and meaningful specific responses from his partners is left with an empty declaration.

22. Appreciate the nonverbal language you communicate to your partner.

Each of us is conveying signals—direct and indirect, verbal and nonverbal—about what we expect from others, how we wish and wish not to be treated.

Because they are for the most part nonverbal and indirect, we are consciously unaware, often, of the effect we have upon others and they upon us. We set up moods in others and others in us which cause us to react in ways we do not acknowledge. By monitoring our physical sensations we can often detect discrepancies between what we are verbally and nonverbally communicating.

23. Ask for compensation to restore equity and power in a relationship.

A societal sanctioned manner for canceling out acts of inequity, insensitivity and mistreatment is saying, "I am sorry," but this too-often-perfunctory statement does not usually assuage aversive feelings. I have found that when you ask for compensation for inequitable treatment, balance is restored to the relationship which helps disipate aversive feelings toward the partner.

References

1. Allport, G. Preface to Victor E. Frankl's *Man's Search for Meaning*. Washington Square Press, New York, 1964, ix–xv.

2. Arieti, S. Volition and Value: A Study based upon Catatonic Schizophrenia. *Comprehensive Psychiatry 2*, 1961, 74–82.

3. Arieti, S. *The Will to be Human*. Dell Books, New York, 1975.

4. Aronson, E. and J. M. Carlsmith. Effect of the Severity of Threat on the Devaluation of Forbidden Behavior. *J. Abnorm. Soc. Psychol.*, 1963, 66 (6), 584–588.

5. Assagioli, R. *The Act of Will*. Penguin Books, Baltimore, 1974.

6. Auden, W. H. *The English Auden*. Random House, New York, 1977.

7. Bannister, D. Donald Bannister: On Clinical Psychology in Britain. *Psychology Monitor, 9* (7), 1978, 6–7.

8. Barrett, W. *The Irrational Man*. Doubleday Anchor Books, Garden City, N. Y., 1958.

9. Barron F. *Creativity and Personal Freedom*. Van Nostrand Reinhold, Indianapolis, 1968.

10. Berdyaev, N. *The Meaning of the Creative Act*. (Translated by D. Lowrie), Macmillian-Collier, New York, 1955.

11. Bernstein, A. The Fear of Compassion. In B. B. Wolman (ed.), *Success and Failure in Psychoanalysis and Psychotherapy*. Macmillan, New York, 1972, 160–176.

12. Bieri, J. Complexity-Simplicity as a Personality Variable in Cognitive and Preferential Behavior. In D. W. Fiske and S. R. Maddi (eds.), *Functions of Varied Experience*. Dorsey Press, Homewood, Ill., 1961.

13. Bieri, J. and E. Blacker. The Generality of Cognitive Complexity in the Perception of People and Ink Blots. *J. Abnorm. Soc. Psychol.*, 1956, *53*, 112–117.

14. Breger, L. Conformity as a Function of the Ability to Express Hostility. *J. of Personality*, 1963, *31* (2), 247–257.

15. Bry, A. *Inside Psychotherapy*. Basic Books, New York, 1972.

16. Byron, Lord. *Don Juan*. (eds. T. G. Steffan and E. Steffan). Penguin, Baltimore, 1978.

17. Camus, A. *The Myth of Sisyphus*. Alfred Knopf, New York, 1955.

18. Camus, A. *The Rebel—An Essay on Man in Revolt*. Vintage Books, New York, 1960.

19. Crowne, D. P. and S. Liverant. Conformity Under Varying Conditions of Personal Commitment. *J. Abnorm. Soc. Psychol.*, 1963, 66 (6), 547–555.

20. Davis, C. M. Self-regulation of Diet in Childhood. *11th Educational Journal of London*, 1947, *5*, 37–40.

21. Dunlap, K. A Revision of the Fundamental Law of Habit Formation. *Science, 57*, 1928, 360–362.

22. Eliot, T. S. *The Cocktail Party.* Harcourt, Brace and World, New York, 1950.

23. Elkin, H. On Existentialism, Phenomenology, and Psychoanalysis: Special Book Reviews, *Psychoanalytic Review, 64,* 1977, 551-558.

24. Ellis, A. *Reason and Emotion in Psychotherapy.* Lyle Stuart, New York, 1962.

25. Farber, L. H. *The Ways of the Will.* Harper and Row, New York, 1968.

26. Fenichel, O. *The Psychoanalytic Theory of Neurosis.* W. W. Norton, New York, 1945.

27. Frankl, V. E. Paradoxical Intention: A Logotherapeutic Technique. *American Journal of Psychotherapy, 14,* 1960, 530-535.

28. Frankl, V. E. *Man's Search for Meaning.* Washington Square Press, New York, 1964.

29. Frankl, V. E. *The Will to Meaning.* World, New York, 1969.

30. Frenkel-Brunswik, E. *Else Frenkel-Brunswik: Selected Papers.* International Universities Press, New York, 1974.

31. Freud, S. *Three Contributions to the Theory of Sexuality.* (Translated by A. A. Brill), Nervous and Mental Disease Publications, New York, 1930.

32. Friedman, L. The Struggle in Psychotherapy: Its Influence on Some Theories. *Psychoanalytic Review, 62,* 1975, 455-462.

33. Fromm, E. *Escape from Freedom.* Holt, Rinehart and Winston, New York, 1963.

34. Gilbert, A. R. Whatever Happened to the Will in American Psychology? *Journal of the History of the Behavioral Sciences, 6,* 1970, 52-57.

35. Glasser, W. *Reality Therapy.* Harper and Row, New York, 1965.

36. Goldberg, C. *Encounter: Group Sensitivity Training Experience.* Science House, New York, 1970[a].

37. Goldberg, C. Encounter Group Leadership. *Psychiatry and Social Science Review, 4* (11), 1970[b], 2-8.

38. Goldberg, C. *The Human Circle: An Existential Approach to the New Group Therapies.* Nelson-Hall, Chicago, 1973.

39. Goldberg, C. Peer Influence in Contemporary Group Psychotherapy. In L. R. Wolberg and M. L. Aronson (eds.), *Group Therapy 1975,* Stratton Intercontinental Medical Books, 1975[a], 232-241.

40. Goldberg, C. Termination—A Meaningful Pseudodilemma in Psychotherapy. *Psychotherapy: Theory, Research and Practice, 12,* 1975[b], 341-343.

41. Goldberg, C. *Therapeutic Partnership—Ethical Concerns in Psychotherapy.* Springer, New York, 1977[a].

42. Goldberg, C. The Reality of Human Will: A Concept Worth Reviving. *Psychiatric Annals, 7,* 1977[b], 566-574.

43. Goldberg, C. Review of Herbert S. Strean's *Crucial Issues in Psychotherapy. Canada's Mental Health, 26,* 1978[a], 19-20.

44. Goldberg, C. The Silent Conspiracy Against Recognizing the Therapeutic Struggle. *Division 32* (Division of Humanistic Psychology of the American Psychological Association) *Newsletter, 6,* 1978[b], 4-5.

45. Goldberg, C. *The Utilization and Limitation of Paradoxical Intervention Approaches in Group Psychotherapy.* In L. R. Wolberg and M. L. Aronson (Eds.), *Group Therapy and Family Therapy 1981.* Brunner-Mazel, New York, 1981.

References

46. Goldberg, C. A Theory of Emotions—Emotionality as the Intentionality of the Self. *Journal of Contemporary Psychotherapy.* (In press).

47. Goldberg, C. *Masters of the Therapeutic Arts.* (Manuscript in preparation).

48. Groddeck, G. *The Meaning of Illness.* International Universities Press, New York, 1977.

49. Groesbeek, C. J. and B. Taylor. The Psychiatrist as Wounded Physician. *American Journal of Psychoanalysis, 37,* 1977, 131–139.

50. Gurdjieff, G.I. *Meetings With Remarkable Men.* Dutton, New York, 1974.

51. Haley, J. *Strategies of Psychotherapy.* Grune and Stratton, New York, 1963.

52. Heidegger, M. *Being and Time.* Harper and Row, New York, 1962.

53. Heider, Fritz. *The Psychology of Interpersonal Relations.* John Wiley, New York, 1957.

54. Hoffman, M. L. Conformity as a Defense Mechanism and a form of Resistance to Genuine Group Influence. *J. of Personality,* 1957, *25,* 412–424.

55. Hora, T. Existential Psychiatry and Group Psychotherapy. In G. M. Gazda (ed.), *Basic Approaches to Group Psychotherapy and Group Counseling.* 2nd edition. C. C. Thomas, Springfield, Ill., 1975.

56. Howard, J. *Please Touch.* McGraw-Hill, New York, 1970.

57. Husserl, E. *The Idea of Phenomenology.* Martinus Wijhoff, The Hague, 1964.

58. Illich, I. *Medical Nemesis: The Expropriation of Health.* Pantheon Books, New York, 1976.

59. Jones, W. T. *A History of Western Philosophy.* 5 volumes. Harcourt, Brace and World, New York, 1969.

60. Jordan, M. Behavioral Forces that are a Function of Attitudes and of Cognitive Organization. *Human Relations, 6,* 1953, 273–287.

61. Jourard, S. M. *Disclosing Man to Himself.* Van Nostrand Reinhold Company, New York, 1968.

62. Kernberg, O. Why Some People Can't Love. *Psychology Today, 12* (1), 1978, 54–59.

63. Kierkegaard, S. *Fear and Trembling and Sickness Unto Death.* Doubleday Anchor Books, New York, 1954.

64. Klein, E. B. Stylistic Components of Response as Related to Attitude Change. *Journal of Personality,* 1963, *31* (11), 38–51.

65. Knight, R. P. Determinism, "Freedom," and Psychotherapy. *Psychiatry, 9,* 1946, 251–262.

66. Kohut, H. Introspection, Empathy and Psychoanalysis. *Journal of the American Psychoanalytic Association, 7,* 1959, 459–483.

67. Kohut, H. *The Restoration of Self.* International Universities Press, New York, 1977.

68. Kopp, S. *If You Meet the Buddha on the Road, Kill Him!* Science and Behavioral Books, Ben Lomond, California, 1972.

69. Kutner, B. Patterns of Mental Functioning Associated with Prejudice in Children. *Psychol. Monographs,* 1958, 72 (7 Whole No. 460), 48 pp.

70. Laing, R. Ontological Insecurity. In H. M. Ruitenbeek (ed.) *Psychoanalysis and Existential Philosophy.* E. P. Dutton, New York, 1962, 41–69.

71. Lapsley, J. N. The Concept of Will. In Lapsley, J. N. (ed.) *The Concept of Willing.* Abingdon Press, Nashville, Tenn., 1967.

72. Lasch, C. *The Culture of Narcissism*. Norton and Company, New York, 1978.

73. Levenson, E. *The Fallacy of Understanding*. Basic Books, New York, 1972.

74. Lindner, R. *The Fifty Minute Hour*. Rinehardt and Company, New York, 1955.

75. Linthorst, J. The Transactional Dimension of Action. *Psychotherapy: Theory, Research and Practice, 12,* 1975, 160–163.

76. Low, A. A. *Mental Health Through Will-training*. Christopher Publishing House, North Quincy, Mass., 1952.

77. Macquarrie, J. Will and Existence. In J. N. Lapsley (ed.), *The Concept of Willing*. Abingdon Press, Nashville, Tenn., 1967.

78. Maddi, S. The Existential Neurosis. *Journal of Abnormal Psychology, 72,* 1967, 311–325.

79. Marañon, G. *Don Juan*. Espasacalpe, Madrid, 1940.

80. Marin, P. The New Narcissism. *Harpers, 251* (1505), 1975, 45–70.

81. Maslow, A. H. *Toward a Psychology of Being*. Van Nostrand Reinhold, New York, 1962.

82. May, R. *Love and Will*. Dell Books, New York, 1974.

83. May, R. Freedom, Determinism and the Future. *Psychology* (April 1977), 6–9.

84. Mazer, M. The Therapeutic Function of the Belief in Will. *Psychiatry, 23,* 1960, 45–52.

85. Menninger, K. *The Theory of Psychoanalytic Technique*. Basic Books, New York, 1958.

86. Miller, G. A. On Turning Psychology Over to the Unwashed. *Psychology Today, 3,* 1969, 127–132.

87. Molina, T. de. *Don Juan: The Beguiler from Seville and the Stone Guest*. (Translated by Max Oppenheimer). Coronado Press, 1976.

88. Mullahy, P. Will, Choice and Ends. *Psychiatry, 12,* 1949, 379–386.

89. Mullan, H. Transference-Countertransference: New Horizons. *International Journal of Group Psychotherapy, 5,* 1955, 169–180.

90. Neitzsche, F. *The Philosophy of Nietzsche*. The Modern Library, New York, 1954.

91. Ofman, W. V. *Affirmation and Reality*. Western Psychological Services, Los Angeles, 1976.

92. Older, J. Four Taboos That May Limit the Success of Psychotherapy. *Psychiatry, 40,* 1977, 197–204.

93. Ormont, L. The Treatment of Pre-oedipal Resistances in the Group Setting. *Psychoanalytic Review, 61,* 1974, 429–441.

94. Ortega y Gassett. *Dehumanization of Art and other Essays on Art, Culture and Literature*. Princeton University Press, Princeton, N. J. 1969.

95. Ovid. *Metamorphoses*. (Translated by Mary Innes), Baltimore, Penguin Books, 1955.

96. Pascal, B. *Pensées*. (Edited and translated by G. B. Rawlings). The Peter Pauper Press, Mount Vernon, N. Y., 1946.

97. Piaget, J. Will and Action. *Bulletin of the Menninger Clinic, 26,* 1962, 138–145.

98. Pirandello, L. *Six Characters in Search of an Author.* In L. Pirandello, *Naked Masks.* E. P. Dutton, New York, 1952, 211–276.

99. Pratt, D. Teh Don Juan Myth. *American Imago, 17,* 1960, 321–335.

100. Rabkin, R. *Strategic Psychotherapy.* Basic Books, New York, 1977.

101. Rank, O. *Will Therapy and Truth and Reality.* Alfred A. Knopf, New York, 1945.

102. Rank, O. *The Don Juan Legend.* (Translated and edited, with an Introduction by D. G. Winter). Princeton University Press, Princeton, N.J., 1975.

103. Reik, T. *Psychology of Sex Relations.* Grove Press, New York, 1945.

104. Riegel, K. F. The Dialectics of Human Development. *American Psychologist, 31,* 1976, 689–700.

105. Roback, A. A. *A History of American Psychology.* Collier Books, New York, 1964.

106. Rohrbaugh, M., H. Tennen, S. Press, L. White, P. Raskin and M. R. Prekering. *Paradoxical Strategies in Psychotherapy.* A Symposium presented at the American Psychological Assoication Annual Conference, San Francisco, August 1977.

107. Rokeach, M. *Open and Closed Mind.* Basic Books, New York, 1960.

105. Rosen, J. *Direct Analysis.* Grune and Stratton. New York, 1953.

109. Rosenthal, R. *Experimenter Effects in Behavior Research.* Halsted Press, New York, 1976.

110. Royce, J. E. Historical Aspects of Free Choice. *Journal of the History of the Behavioral Science, 6,* 1970, 48–51.

111. Ruitenbeek, H. M. *The New Group Therapies.* Avon Books, New York, 1970.

112. Salzman, L. Will and the Therapeutic Process. *American Journal of Psychoanalysis, 34,* 1974, 277–290.

113. Sartre, J. *Being and Nothingness.* Philosophical Library, New York, 1956.

114. Schopenhauer, A. *The World as Will and Idea.* Dover Press, New York, 1966.

115. Shur, M. *Freud: Living and Dying.* International Universities Press, New York, 1972.

116. Schutz, W. C. *Here Comes Everybody.* Harper and Row, New York, 1971.

117. Sears, R. R., E. E. Maccoby and H. Levin. *Patterns of Child Rearing.* Row, Peterson, Evanston, Ill., 1957.

118. Sexton, L. G. and L. Ames (eds.), *Anne Sexton: A Self-portrait in Letters.* Houghton-Mifflin, Boston, 1977.

119. Schaffer R. Talking to Patients in psychotherapy. Bulletin of the Menninger Clinic, 1974, *38* (6), 503–515.

120. Shaffer, P. *Equus. A Play.* Avon Books, New York, 1975.

121. Shainberg, D. Dialogues with Knishnamurti. An unpublished description of the Indian philosopher's ideas. 1978.

122. Shaw, G. B. *Man and Superman.* Penguin Books, Baltimore.

123. Shelly, P. *Adonais. A Poem.* O. Williams (ed.), *Immortal Poems of the English Language.* Pocket Books, New York, 1956, 306–320.

124. Shepard, M. and M. Lee. *Games Analysts Play.* G. P. Putnam and Sons, New York, 1970.

125. Skinner, B. F. *Beyond Freedom and Dignity.* Alfred A. Knopf, New York, 1971.

126. Small, L. *The Briefer Psychotherapies.* Brunner/Mazel, New York, 1971.

127. Smith, K. H. Ego Strength and Perceived Competence as Conformity Variables. *J. Abnorm. Soc. Psych.,* 1961, *62* (1), 169–171.

128. Solomon, R. C. *The Passions.* Doubleday Anchor Books, Garden City, N. Y., 1977.

129. Sponitz, H. *Psychotherapy of Pre-oedipal Conditions.* Jason Aronson, New York, 1976.

130. Stampfl, T. G. and D. J. Levis. Essentials of Implosive Therapy: A Learning-theory Psychodynamic Behavioral Therapy. *Journal of Abnormal Psychology, 72,* 1977, 496–503.

131. Strean, H. The Contribution of Paradigmatic Psychotherapy to Psychoanalysis. *Psychoanalytic Review, 51,* 1964, 365–381.

132. Sugarman, S. Sin and Madness: A Transformation of Consciousness. *Psychoanalytic Review, 61,* 1974, 497–516.

133. Sylvester, J. J. Quote attributed to Sylvester in *Comprehensive Psychology,* 1978, *23,* 486.

134. Taft, J. *Otto Rank: A Biographical Study.* Julian Press, New York, 1958.

135. Thomas, L. *The Lives of a Cell: Notes of a Biology Watcher.* Viking Press, New York, 1974.

136. Tourney, G. Review of *The Narcissistic Condition:* A Fact of our Lives and Times. Edited by Marie Coleman Nelson. *American Jouranl of Psychiatry, 135,* 1978, 765–766.

137. Vassiliou, G. and V.G. Vassiliou. Introducing Disequilibrium in Group Therapy. In L.R. Wolberg and M.L. Aronson (Eds.), *Group Therapy 1976.* Stratton Intercontinental Medical Book Corporation, New York, 1976.

138. Venzetti, B. Last Speech to the Court. In S. Rodman (ed.), *A New Antholgoy of Modern Poetry* (rev. ed.), Modern Library, New York, 1946, 106–107.

139. Watson, J. B. *Behavior.* Henry Holt, New York, 1914.

140. Watts, A. *Psychotherapy East and West.* Ballantine Books, New York, 1961.

141. Watzlawick, P., J. Weakland and R. Fisch. *Change: Principles of Problem Formation and Problem Resolution.* W. W. Norton, New York, 1974.

142. Weinstein, L. *The Metamorphoses of Don Juan.* Stanford University Press, Palo Alto, Calif., 1959.

143. Weisman, A. D. *The Existential Core of Psychoanalysis.* Little, Brown and Company, Boston, 1965.

144. Wheelis, A. Will and Psychoanalysis. *Journal of the American Psychoanalytic Association, 4,* 1956, 285–303.

145. Wheelis, A. *The Desert.* Basic Books, New York, 1970.

146. Whitaker, C. Struggling with Impotent Impasse: Absurdity and Acting-in. *Journal of Marriage and Family Counseling, 4,* 1978, 69–77.

147. Whitaker, D., and M. Lieberman. *Psychotherapy Through Group Process.* Atherton Press, New York, 1967.

148. Wilson, R. N. Albert Camus–Personality as Creative Struggle. In R. W. White (ed.), *The Study of Lives, Essays on Personality in Honor of Henry A. Murray.* Atherton, N.Y., 1963, chapter 15.

149. Winter, D. *The Power Motive.* The Free Press, New York, 1963.

150. Winter, D. Introduction. *The Don Juan Legend* by Otto Rank. (Translated, with an Introduction by D. Winter). Princeton University Press, Princeton, N. J., 1975.

151. Wolpe, J. *Psychotherpay by Reciprocal Inhibition.* Stanford University Press, Palo Alto, 1958.

152. Worthington, M. Don Juan as Myth. *Literature and Psychology, 12,* 1962, 113–124.

153. Yalom, I. D. *The Theory and Practice of Group Psychotherapy.* Basic Books, New York, 1970.

Index